The Lone Pine Ranch

The Lone Pine Ranch

Maurice Graves Emery

iUniverse, Inc.
New York Lincoln Shanghai

The Lone Pine Ranch

iUniverse, Inc.

For information address:
iUniverse, Inc.
2021 Pine Lake Road, Suite 100
Lincoln, NE 68512
www.iuniverse.com

ISBN: 0-595-28541-4

Printed in the United States of America

Contents

Preface

A degree of interest in pioneering the West of any locality in which one lives is enviable. As time passes, more interest is, therefore, attached to it. Hopefully, it will awaken old-timers, and those descended from Pioneer stock. Determination and untiring efforts put forth by Pilgrim Fathers who desired to find a better way of life.

This book offers no fiction from a religious or scientific standpoint, nor in poise of a hero, or self praise. It is simple in style and diction.

The conclusion brings the closing incidents down to a recent date and finishes in brief the biography of Maurice Graves Emery. Memories and imagination are great contributors to personal values and consideration for humankind. This story is about a long life of more than eighty-six years.

1

This story begins at an early age when Maurice remembers the events that happened as he grew and matured. These events have remained vivid in his memory as though they had happened yesterday. Maurice remembers his parents were working for Bill Kittredge in northern Klamath County, Oregon on a ranch during the winter of 1918. The main Klamath Marsh Ranch was, at that time, one half mile from the military crossing. Winter supplies were hauled from Klamath Falls to that Location; and one of the main staples was squash, easily kept during the long hard winter. Seeds from the squash were fed to squirrels when they came out of hibernation. The snow was exceptionally deep and the cattle were fed from a horse drawn sled. Everyone was snowed in and stayed at this location for five long hard months. It was, indeed, a hard winter.

Everett Arthur Emery and Esther Graves Emery

On May 26,1918, Clifford Dale Emery was born to Esther Graves Emery and Everett Arthur Emery. Soon after the birth of Dale, Everett, known as "Slivers," moved his family from Klamath Marsh to the one hundred sixty acre homestead west of Silver Lake, Oregon, which Slivers had previously homesteaded. The house was a three room house built from board and bat siding. The lumber was rough lumber from the Embody sawmill nearby. After getting his family settled in the house, Slivers went to Summer Lake to finish his work for Bill Kittredge. Water was supplied to the house by a well which was dug with pick and shovel, as were most water supplies in that part of the country. Wooden covers, with a lid for easy access to the water supply below, were necessary. One sunny morning, from inside the house, there was thought to be a noise sounding like that lid was being used for something other than water. Observation disclosed that Maurice had thrown a cat down the well. In an attempt to rescue the animal with a rope tied to the bucket, no one was able to rescue the cat before it drowned. The following day Mother and Maurice, aged two years and Dale, aged six months, departed the premises, and joined Slivers in Summer Lake where he was working as a ranch hand for Mr. Kittredge at the River Ranch in Summer Lake. Undoubtedly the cat's remains buried at thirty feet deep is probably the deepest cat grave in Lake County, Oregon. Slivers moved his family into the house on River Ranch which was substantially better than the board and batten homestead house. This house was their abode for only a short time. The house was forty feet from the banks of Ana River. There was no modern plumbing. This was a place that required adult supervision in order that Maurice and Dale would not fall into that whirlpool water. Ranch hands broke sod, hauled manure and built dams to flood irrigate the meadow lands. Wagons with dump boards, drawn by horses, were used to better dump the loads.

2

Mother, with a half broke team of mules, all alone, drove six miles to the Summer Lake store to get a new Damascus sewing machine previously ordered from a Montgomery ward catalog. Mother arrived safely back at the ranch with the machine safely tied down. The two young boys, Maurice and Dale, had a new toy. The machine's treadle was a great plaything when their mother was not nearby.

Maurice, Dale, and Kenneth, 1926

Slivers and Esther, looking forward to something more than a meager wage, were about to do what, they thought, would be their last move. They made a much deliberated decision to move on and become cattle barons, if possible. They loaded two horse drawn wagons, two small boys, and all their possessions. Mattresses were piled high atop the rear wagon. The long twenty plus miles to the Lone Pine Ranch and beyond the second rest period at Picture Rock Pass, they rested their steeds within fifty feet of the now famous petroglyphs. Winding their way onward, over crooked dirt roads, they reached the Lone Pine Ranch before dark. The ranch was named Lone Pine, because it had a single pine tree, three feet in diameter and approximately eighty feet high.

Lone Pine Ranch House

When they arrived at the new location, the new tenants were greeted by Felix Duncan and Pernicia Taylor. Pernicia, a former dance hall girl from Reno, Nevada, was the housekeeper for Felix. The lonely country on the east side of Silver Lake was presently a dry lake bed. There were many passersby both daytime and during the nights. The road was a main thoroughfare between Silver Lake and Lakeview. One night, Pernicia, alone in the house, heard a knock at the door. With some fear and foreboding she opened the door and found a man affronting her. However, the man meant no harm and was hungry; so she gave him some food and he departed. Later she exclaimed "If he had attacked me, I would have grabbed my long Spanish Stiletto and stabbed his guts out."

Felix had recently purchased a new model T Ford. He was unable to distinguish the combination of the three pedals on the floor (brake, reverse and clutch). He built a new garage to house his newly purchased vehicle. Still unsure of the pedals, he installed doors on both ends of the garage. This enabled him to exit from either end of the building in case he pushed the wrong pedal.

Behind the property were rim rocks 400 feet high. Duncan and Elmer Lutz had previously built a dam for irrigation. The dam to harness 241 acre feet of water thereby harnessing Duncan Creek. Lutz, for his part, blasted and dug a ditch to his nearby 320 acre spread. The rocky ditch was called Lutz Cut. The ranch was an overnight stop for passersby. There were many wagons hauling freight. Settled for the night, horses were cared for, the wagon wheels were lubricated with axle grease. Axle grease, in that part of the country, at that time, originated in Yreka, California. The ranch was located on the road to Lakeview, the county seat. The nearest town of significant size was Bend, Oregon, eighty miles in a northerly direction.

The Emery family, at this juncture, was only partially settled in. Mr. Duncan had built a wooden flume near the mouth of Duncan Creek. The flume was constructed with one inch by twelve inch rough sawn lumber. The boards were nailed together in a U shape, which, in turn would, when full, send the roaring water to a ditch. The hand dug ditch carried the water behind the barn and living quarters to two fields of alfalfa consisting of approximately forty acres which was flood irrigated.

The next move was to buy livestock if the cattle baron idea was to succeed. Mr. Emery purchased the Frank Bass herd. Some of which were dairy cows. The Lone Pine barn also had facilities for milk production. Mr. Bass was willing to sell. The creamery at Silver Lake was in the process of closing its doors. This was disruptive to Mr. Bass. Mrs. Emery continued to send cream to the facility until its final closure. Immediately following the cattle purchase, other animals and poultry were needed i.e. a few piglets, and horses. Dick, the one and only wheel horse and Midget, the mare for riding. Dick was used to pull the buggy to and from town. When surrounded by the shavs of the buggy, with harness affixed to the singletree, whip on the dashboard, Dick was a real prancing animal. Town was nine miles from the ranch. The railroad was to be extended from Shaniko, Oregon, to Silver Lake, Oregon. The plan for the extension of the railroad was abandoned, which caused great disappointment for everyone.

Hundreds came to that high desert country anticipating a better way of life i.e. Charles Mitchell from New York City and Albert Johnson, from Australia. Farming was their ultimate goal. Others came to provide services. Sixty-one single men relocated in the Silver Lake area. As a result, men outnumbered women by more than four to one. Simultaneously, homes and businesses sprang up like weeds in a flower bed. Two hotels, Mrs Manning's rooming house and the Chrisman Hotel, owner, Mr. Chrisman. A newspaper, Silver Lake Leader, two pool halls, a butcher shop, grocery and Linebaugh & Groth general merchandise whose inventory included horse drawn rakes and mowing machines. Mr. Chrisman was a rock solid entrepreneur and devout business man. Due to the high altitude of the area, and short growing season, he decided to invent a blower to warm the air, thereby, increasing crop yields. He remodeled a threshing machine and affixed a wood burning stove on one end. The idea was to stoke the wood burner with firewood, install a gasoline engine to run the blower and that would, ultimately, warm the cold air hovering above the existing plantings. However, the new invention was less than successful. Mr. Chrisman's dream was abandoned and the contraption was stored in a building across the street from his hotel until the mid 1920's. There were approximately thirty-five ranchers and homesteaders in the area of Silver Lake, also known as Paulina Valley. Located west of Silver Lake, were seven ranches located at Antelope flat. A single man, Claude Trowbridge, was a carpenter and musician. His musical performances were heard far and wide. His instruments included mouth harp, drums and violin. His posture, ability, music and good nature contributed a great deal to his fellow men. Located three miles beyond Antelope Flat, there was another flat surrounded by trees called Bear Flat. Bear Flat had a halfway stopover ran by H. B. Mckinley. Cattle drovers, on their way to Klamath Marsh and beyond, spent time at this location. Accommodations were not the best around. Horse manure in the barn was seldom removed-if ever. The bedding was used over and over by drovers. Whenever anyone washed and dried his face, they looked in a far corner of the towel to find the least soiled spot that had not been blackened by previous users. The next morning, he ate hot cakes and oat meal before moving on. Needless to say, many gallons of moonshine were removed from Bear Flat and Antelope Flat during the Prohibition Days, at about five dollars a gallon to the drinker. A Mr. Foster from Silver Lake, was a go between producers of the above mentioned gallons, and the thirsty population around the area. He purchased a new Reo Flying Cloud automobile, indeed a very nice one. He was quite a sight, with only one arm, he manipulated that automobile with style and finesse.

3

Oscar Parrein was the local blacksmith and a good one. He could remove the wheel spokes, install new ones, shrink the iron bands with heat and water, assuring a customer of its satisfactory road ability. Oscar was a Belgian, birthplace unknown. Automobiles were coming into the area and mechanics were not to be found under every sagebrush. His burning desire was to become an automobile mechanic. However, he was less than successful. When approached by a road weary motorist with a problem, he would say "Me fixem." From Blacksmith to auto mechanic, even today, would be difficult for the average blacksmith. Consequently, the motorist was stranded and distraught until someone with the knowledge and ability to repair a Horseless Carriage arrived upon the scene. Oscar finally left town and his destination was never known.

Adin McCall: Previous to this writer's knowledge, one story as told. Adin and his cronies came out of the Shamrock pool hall to see the first newly arrived motor vehicle. Automobiles in those days were called Horseless Carriages. Adin chortled: "If that damn thing will move without a horse pulling it, I will lie down and let it run over me." That he did, the wheels passed over his legs. No harm done. Mr. Gephart: from whence he came, this writer is unaware. Mr. Gephart had a more modern freight and passenger service. Gasoline powered vehicles to traverse the winding, dusty, rutted and lonely road from Bend, Oregon, to Southern Lake County, were now in use. The mail service was much improved as was passenger service. Those hardy souls living in the area, at that time, excluding this writer, should be forever congratulated. The stagecoach passed through, carrying passengers, mail and various items i.e. dogs, cats, or whatever. Canvas bags carrying mail were tossed from the moving vehicle onto the yard of each resident along the way. Residents removed their mail and placed the mail sack in a convenient location. The stagecoach driver, when returning, would pick up the sack and return it to the Post Office in Silver Lake for the next routine delivery.

That part of the country was blessed with telephone service. However, those with a telephone had a wall hung, battery powered, hand crank type. The bare wire phone lines were above ground atop a high pole. Glass insulators on top of each pole carrying the wire, provided insulation from the wood pole which would have grounded out the signal. In order to call out, you used a series of long and short signals. One half turn on the hand crank was considered a short. Two or more turns were considered a long. If your cousin lived several miles from you; and his signal was two shorts and a long, you would turn the crank two half turns with a short pause between the two rings. After the second short, another pause, then two or more turns you would hear your cousin's voice. Everyone on the circuit could hear his neighbor's signal. The ring at the Lone Pine Ranch was three longs.

The ranch was along the shores of Silver Lake; and the lake had recently gone dry No water! Now, a lakebed consisting of eight thousand plus acres was potentially a haven for ranching and farming. Land hungry squatters invaded the lakebed. There were thirty-eight abodes, most of which, were one and two-room wooden structures. Their visions of prosperity were short lived. Oregon laws stipulated that when a body of water ceased to exist, residents with on shore deeds surrounding the now dry lake bed were entitled to fence to the center for personal use. The wooden structures were removed and the owners of deeded land fenced to the center. This writer distinctly remembers only three of the squatters. The Cox family, Russell Emery, a single man, and Ole Olton, a single man. Olton had purchased a new iron wheeled Fordson tractor which was stored at Lone Pine. He left his one room abode, which was removed from the lake bed by Dave Mosby who commenced homestead proceedings at Owl Creek. Mr. Mosby also turned tail and ran. Mr. Mosby's supposed empire also crumbled and his abode was used as a wood shed at Lone Pine for many years.

4

In 1921, Mrs. Emery drove her recently purchased second hand Model T Ford to Mrs. McCrackin's sale at Christmas Lake. The auction was a disaster, due to hard times. Limited patronage and a lack of money forced many to liquidate in a hurry. However, mother bought a forty-eight inch round table for one dollar and other items for the ranch back at Lone Pine. The table was a bargain.

Christmas Lake, during the early nineteen hundreds, was almost a total disaster. Families moved away due to drought conditions. Many ate their breakfast, left their cooking utensils, knives and forks on their tables and walked away completely discouraged. This was in 1921. The Buchanan family, Woods family and Henry Hatch, a single man, remained for several years.

In the interim, back at Lone Pine, fences were built and native grasses were, in most places, waist high Rich soil was an inducement to plant grain for cattle feed. Rye hay, seven feet tall, stacked for winter feeding was a godsend for the cattle men The climate was best suited for rye hay. Piglets and chickens were fast becoming pork and eggs in that order. Milk was already in abundance. Something more than milk, pork and eggs was about to arrive. Mother came home from a nearby home, carrying a basket which she placed on the table she had purchased from the McCracken sale in 1921. Standing on chairs and looking in the basket, Maurice and Dale saw a fat little baby boy. His name was Kenneth Emery. That was August 6, 1922. He had, when hungry, the voice of a bull moose stranded in the woods. Many times the youngest in any family is more spoiled than the older ones. Our next door neighbors to the north were the Oliver Hill family. Mrs. Hill was a daughter of F. M. Chrisman, hotel owner. The Hill's had two daughters, Cecile and Caroline. The Hill's left their homestead and moved to Portland in 1925.

Neighbors to the south, Adin and Gertrude McCall had three children. Chester was the older one; and Fern and Lynn were born later. Chester rode his bicycle nine miles to Silver Lake School over a rough, rocky, rutty road. After his Silver Lake schooling, he went to college where he met his future wife, Betty. After finishing college, they relocated in New York City.

5

Silver Lake, Oregon was only one of many places throughout Oregon to be settled during the early 1900s. The Wardwell family, from a distant location, settled one half mile from Silver Lake. Their departure from the area took them to San Francisco, California. Mr. Wardwell worked in a commercial bank. His position there is unknown at this time. Their home in Silver Lake was later purchased by E. G. Graves. Mr. Graves abandoned his livery stable business. Automobiles were becoming a reality. The use of horse drawn wagons and buggies was on the decline. A huge amount of money was missing from the San Francisco bank where Burt Wardwell was employed. Yes, embezzled-stolen. The thieves positioned themselves as trustworthy. Conspirators they were, indeed. They placed the thievery on Burt Wardwell. Wardwell, well knew, he wasn't involved. However, the jury found him guilty. The stolen money was not to be found. Wardwell was convicted and imprisoned on Alcatraz for fifteen years. During time on the "Island Hotel," he told about many horror stories. One of the more significant one's was the bed-bug paintings on the prison walls. Bed bugs, after sucking fresh blood from sleeping inmates, were found throughout the area. Inmates would place a finger on a full rounded bed bug, squish the blood and draw pictures on the walls opposite their "bug bitten cellmates," who were asleep. The food, at times, consisted of bread and water only. Unsophisticated odors were prevalent and unbearable. Dirty socks and most clothing needed immediate attention. Mr. Wardwell was taught the art of taxidermy while incarcerated

Meanwhile, Mrs. Wardwell was working feverishly to clear her husband's name and get him home where he belonged. Her dedication was unrelenting during those years. After spending huge amounts of money on attorney fees, her efforts were finally rewarded. Burt Wardwell was released from prison. The real culprits were located through the efforts of Mrs. Wardwell's attorneys. Burt was released from the infamous Alcatraz Island with only a cougar hide rug under his arm.

The Wardwell's, with the cougar hide, returned to Silver Lake in 1925. The cougar hide rug was eight feet long when spread on the floor at Lone Pine. The head was fully mounted. It's mouth wide open, with teeth clearly visible and ready for a kill. Indeed, a beautiful specimen. Mr. Wardwell presented the cougar rug to mother as a special gift. The mischievous Emery boys, when mother wasn't around, found the cougar to be a wonderful play thing. They would drape the rug over their bodies. The head, protruding forward, would appear to be a vicious beast. They approached the family dogs. The dogs were in an uproar. A piece of the nose was bitten off by "Rover." The boys took the cougar back into the house and spread it out on the living room floor. Mother never knew why her beautiful master piece suffered the loss of part of its nose.

6

The Osmussin family lived one mile east of Silver Lake on a small dry-land farm. The family, distressed as many people were, decided to utilize their favorite horse for a unique power source. A twelve foot pole was affixed horizontally to a vertical pole buried deep in the ground. The vertical pole and the horizontal pole came together above ground level. Two worm gears, one on top where the poles intersected and one near ground level. The ground level one went horizontally to a washing machine. Electricity was not available. The horse, Fern, was prepared to provide power for a community laundering facility. Fern stood at the outer end of the horizontal pole. Tethered below the far end, old Fern would go around in a twenty-four foot circle. When Fern stopped, a stern reminder, command or otherwise was administered by Mrs. Osmussin. That was undoubtedly the only horse driven carousel washing machine in Lake County. Blowing cold north wind, drought conditions and less than anticipated profit from the horse driven washing machine was most discouraging. The Osmussins' made a decision. Get out of here!

Soon after the departure of the Osmussin family to "Parts unknown", the Judd family occupied the premises. Lloyd and Mrs. Judd had a son, Leon. Leon was a young man small in stature and a tough prize fighter. He was known as "Battling Judd." When boxing in the ring with an opponent of similar size and weight, he was hard to defeat. He was well known in the area, and also, well advertised. The washing machine at that location was, once again, less than profitable. The Judds' tenure in Silver Lake proved less than profitable. The axles on their wagon were well greased. Their thoughts were also well greased. "Let's get the hell out of here!" The wagon was loaded with all their possessions. The horse driven washing machine was left behind. The Judd family was ready to move. Their destination was somewhere in Nevada. Their new location was never known.

7

The Lone Pine Ranch in Lake County was where the Lone Pine cattle were cared for during the winter months each year. Summer pasture was needed. Slivers had his eye on a ranch (owned by the Indians), at Klamath Marsh, soon to be for sale. Klamath Marsh is on the Klamath Indian Reservation. Indians lived there the year around. Indians had difficulties, at times, amongst themselves. Knight's ranch was adjacent to Eugene Isaac's ranch. Animosity between Knight and Isaac prompted Isaac to terminate Knight's successful ranching business. Knight had purchased two new horse drawn wooden wheeled wagons and other equipment. Isaac, with a double bit woodsman's axe went to the Knight Ranch and chopped the spokes out of every wheel. Knight was in town for a few days when the incident occurred. Wheel hubs, spokes and twisted metal were strewn about. Knight sold his ranch to Frank Bolliger. Further harassment was not forthcoming.

Bolliger, a former resident of Wright City, Missouri, was a brute of a man. He was a single man, a perfectionist, and proud of his many accomplishments. Miles of new fences were built with posts in perfect alignment The fence braces were deep in the ground. His barbed wire was as tight as a fiddle string. Following a hard days work he would prepare his own home cooked dinner. Pots, pans and dishes were sparkling clean. When the kitchen was clean, he would stand in front of the kitchen sink and fall sound asleep. Awakening from his deep sleep, he would demonstrate his shaving ability with his highly sharpened double bit axe. It was honed to perfection, competitive with a razor blade. Whiskers would fall to the floor on which he was standing. One of his greater undertakings was to stand flat footed behind one of his horse drawn wagons and with his hands behind his back, sink his teeth into a hundred pound sack of grain lifting it onto the wagon. Many local residents witnessed his tremendous strength. Bolliger was an admirable man with no known enemies. His trustworthiness was never questioned by anyone.

A few miles from the Bolliger Ranch, another new rancher appeared on the scene. His name was George Hoyt. George had previously been a gardener in one of the larger California cities. He was, at that time, unaware of the harsh climate in Klamath County at forty-six hundred foot elevation. A small herd of cattle and other well known animals were purchased as part of the ranch. George was famous for his grammar. He twisted his words around, dramatically. Those who knew him never understood his tactics. Was he changing words to entertain his friends or not? George decided to plant potatoes. Potatoes are easily kept in the cellar during the long severe winter months. Average people, with a common knowledge of the English language, who found their crops being jeopardized by severe elements, would say "The altitude is too high, the potatoes won't mature." George would say "The multitude is too high, the potatoes won't manure." He further stated "Too damn cold here! I, too, am leaving this country."

8

Herman Seaman and son, Cecil, were camped near the Kittredge Ranch at Abraham flat. They settled in for the winter. Plentiful supplies of canned milk, coffee, flour, baking powder and other staples were in the camp. They were prepared to endure for the entire winter, if necessary. The small cabin was their abode. Trapping coyotes for their furs was their goal. Steel leg traps, well disguised, were placed nearby a dead carcass. Urine was extracted from a previous kill, placed in a small bottle and carried by the trappers. The scent was sometimes placed near a bush or tree. The trap, also well disguised, was placed nearby to catch the, wild, cunning and curious coyote. The Seamans' successes were attributed to their previous knowledge of hunting and trapping in the most northern states. Coyote fur was stripped from each carcass nearby the disguised trap placement. Furs were carried to the cabin. Skis and or snowshoes were under each foot. Burlap sacks were loaded over each man's shoulder with the furs. When the trappers arrived home, the furs were cleaned and stretched over two boards. The two stretching boards were approximately thirty-six inches in length. Boards were three inches wide and rounded on the ends. The two rounded ends were extended to the head of each fur from the rear. The bottoms of the boards were spread with a smaller board and a series of nails and holes. The stretching was in proportion to the size of each fur. Hanging from the walls of the cabin to dry and cure were their prized possessions. Following the winter kill, furs would be shipped to furriers for further processing. Ladies of the land were overjoyed. with new fur coats. Near the end of the trapping season, "Coyote"Moore and an accomplice approached the lonely cabin. Their guns were drawn. Their mission was robbery. The bed clothing and mattresses were thrown outside in the snow. Herman and Cecil were tied, spread eagled on the cold bed springs. Their hands and feet were wired to the bedsprings. Doors were left open for both to freeze to death. The furs were gone! Agonizing moments followed. They were left to die.

The thieves had not wired one of Cecil's hands sufficiently tight. He was able, with much effort, to pull one hand through the wire. In doing so, skin was torn from most of his right hand. The hostages were free. Country wide, residents knew those men, worked with them and agonized over the permanent scars over most of Cecil's right hand. He died at the age of twenty-five. Coyote Moore and his accomplice were subsequently released from jail. Moore, in another routine adventure, was driving alone near where the robbery had taken place at Abraham Flat. Sub-zero temperatures caused his car to stall. Without heat or sufficient clothing, his life was being jeopardized. Because of the light blowing snow, poor visibility and inability to walk the great distance for help; he made the last decision of his life. Stay with the car was his choice. He was found frozen to death in his car several days later. The whereabouts of his partner in crime is presently unknown.

9

Older men were interested in seeing the younger one's grow into manhood. Knowing the "facts of life" would be of prime importance to them. When it was apparent that a young man was nearing the age of manhood, older men would take him with them to a local brothel. Inside the brothel the young man would be invited to sit on a very comfortable sofa. The air was filled with the smell of perfume. Somewhat embarrassed, the young man would feel like crawling under one of the sofa cushions or, better yet, under the sofa. He knew what was going to happen next. His companions would say in a clear undertone, "Boy, be brave, don't be a little boy any more." Emotions were running high when the girls single file, strolled from the back room into the reception room These girls were different than girls he knew. They were dressed in fancy dresses, with ribbons and bows in their hair; and they smelled delightful. One of the girls came over and touched his face with her soft hand. The two men watched, in awe, as drops of sweat arose on the boy's forehead. As they watched, the young man and the young working girl left the reception room together. The older men's mission had been accomplished; and they hastily strode back to their nineteen thirty Ford pickup truck. There they waited for the return of the boy; who was now a man. Now there were three men in the pickup, two dogs and three saddles in the rear.

The ranch was one hundred miles down the road. It was a dark and stormy night. When they reached the ranch, they saw that horses were nearby. The cook had a breakfast of steak and eggs prepared. The three men hastily "gulped down" their breakfast; and immediately thereafter, saddles were gingerly placed on the backs of three horses, cinches were tightened, horses were bridled and the dogs were ready to romp over the distant hills in search of lost cattle. Minutes later, they were out of sight. Whorehouses were not a choice word at that time. Ladies of the evening was a better phrase. Working girls do make good company for working men.

10

Edward and Belle Lundy were proprietors of the famous Chrisman Hotel in Silver Lake for many years. The two story hotel was a landmark in the area. Mrs. Lundy was well qualified for such a position. They had three children, Thelma, Leland and Claudis. Adjacent to the hotel, was a butcher shop ran by P. D. Reeder. Choice meats, such as beef, pork, lamb and on special occasions poultry and fish were sold over the counter. The two businesses were formerly ran by Francis M. Chrisman, prior to his departure from the area. The Lundys' were next in line to operate the hotel. The meals were served family style for fifty cents each meal. Not everyone, living today, remembers the hardships suffered by human beings during those deplorable, unexplainable, drastic, complicated depression years. However, the Lundys' charged fifty cents for meals and a dollar a day for a room. The success of the business was due to the efforts of Mrs. Lundy and her daughter, Thelma.

They purchased a new 1930 Marquett automobile. The Marquett, manufactured by General Motors Corporation, was not a great success. The Marquett was manufactured for only two years. There were several automobiles manufactured about the same time. The Erskine, Terraplane, Moon, Reo, Nash, Mormon, Desoto, Whippet, and others too numerous to mention, were seen on the antiquated highways. In all, approximately twenty-two hundred gasoline powered vehicles, supposedly road worthy, have fallen by the wayside. The above mentioned numbers were substantiated, by an article in Reader's Digest as witnessed and read, in nineteen fifty-two. Maurice Ward owned a Terraplane. Leonard Koger, formerly a homesteader in Bear Flat, worked at the Lone Pine, as a cattle feeder during the 1930–31 winter. He had a new Whippet car. The car was parked in a shed behind the barn from Monday to Sunday. Every Sunday morning after the cattle were fed, we harnessed a team of horses and hooked a log chain to the rear of the Whippet and pulled it backward out of the shed. The car was too cold to start on its own. The team pulled the Whippet around the barn yard several times to get it started. Leonard, after feeding cattle, went to Silver Lake to visit his girl friend. He returned late Sunday evening and again parked the Whippet in the shed. The car would remain in the shed until the following Sunday, when the backward ritual would again take place.

Mr. Lundy's contribution to the hotel operation was much less than antici-pated by Mrs. Lundy and her daughter, Thelma. Ed Lundy's "sidekick," Red Morris, was in the area. The two of them, after swallowing prune juice, or other similar liquid, spiked with a well known stimulant, were a couple of "ruthless ruf-fians on the loose." They were the best of friends, however. Whenever the stimu-lant was ingested into their bodies, all Hell broke loose. Both of them would fight furiously toe to toe; and beat their chests, both infuriated at each other. The "slew juice" had both men primed to the hilt. Neither one was ever accused of picking a fight with anyone else

The dancing public, on a Saturday night at the "Odd Fellows Hall," was in full swing. Both Ed and Red were there. It was obvious that Ed and Red were both intoxicated. Both men were in rare form ready to demonstrate their abilities with their fists. Ed grabbed Red by the throat, backed him upright against the wall alongside the wood box, and took aim at his nose. Ed's right hand, fully tightened, was ready for a direct hit. Fortunately for Red, he was a bit less intoxi-cated than Ed. Red saw what was coming. His legs automatically became tight-ened. He slid down the wall. Ed's fist went over the top of that red hair, and his hand crashed into the wall. The wall didn't move. The crowd became silent. The show was over.

Fire leveled the Chrisman Hotel around the mid nineteen thirties. Ed Lundy, after the fire, became the chuck wagon driver and cook for the Chewaucan Land & Cattle Company, more commonly known as the Z X Ranch, until his retire-ment many years later. Ed's wife, Belle retired. Daughter, Thelma, became the wife of Jake Harris. The Harris family lived in Klamath Falls previous to their demise.

11

Many strong, husky and sturdy men were found through out the Silver Lake Community. Women were hard working. Their tolerance for mischievousness was limited. Their heads were held high and they were very protective of their husband and children. There were two men whose activities and actions superseded the more reserved ones. They were Jim Steele and Curtis Donahue. Steele was considered to be a drifter and horseman. His huge frame, while in the saddle, was a cut above the ordinary bronco buster. He was an admirable man. Steele, while riding in Summer Lake during a terrific thunderstorm, appeared and stopped at the Swanton homestead. Both he and his horse were drenched from the pouring rain. Lightning was everywhere. Before he could dismount, a bolt of lightning struck his horse. The horse dropped dead beneath the seat of Steele's pants. Steele walked away from the dead animal unscathed. He was alive and well. The incident was never completely understood. Theories prevailed. One theory was the lightning struck nearby. Another theory was that the horse had steel shoes nailed to the bottom of its hooves. Did the leather in the saddle insulate Steele from immediate death? No one knew!

Curtis Donahue was a stage driver. He hauled passengers, limited freight and mail between Bend and Lakeview for the Hollinshead Stage Line. The stagecoach malfunctioned nine miles South of Silver Lake at the Lone Pine Ranch. Curtis was traveling toward Summer Lake, Paisley and Lakeview, when an accident occurred. He didn't have any passengers on that particular run. The stagecoach left the road, rolled over and landed upside down below a steep embankment. Curtis extricated himself from the vehicle. His chauffeur's cap was not immediately found. He walked the half mile to the Lone Pine. His face was dirty. His hair was disheveled.; and he was distraught and agitated. The old saying, "The mail must go through" still stands. The mail was loaded in the ranch's nineteen twenty-eight Chevrolet. Curtis and Maurice Emery climbed aboard. Maurice drove the ninety miles. The entire ninety miles to Lakeview was a dirt and gravel road. The mail reached its intended destination only two hours late.

Coincidently, Donahue and Steele had one thing in common. Their interests were centered around one lovely lady. The lady attracted many other local men, also. However, both Donahue and Steele were the top contenders. Ultimately, a smoldering threat between the two men occurred. It was tumultuous times for both men, indeed. Steele was bigger and stronger than Donahue. Donahue was faster during an encounter; and he was also a fast thinker. They met, a few ugly words were exchanged; and the show began. Donahue was underpowered. Steele walked home with a grin from ear to ear across his broad face. Donahue was not about to give up. He was emboldened by Steele's slower pace.

Their next meeting was significantly different for only a few brief seconds. Donahue approached Steele with fire in his eyes. He was confident he could win. He was also confident he had Steele where he wanted him-overpowered at last. During the melee, Donahue broke his hand. The pain was excruciating. The last swing at Steele's steel like jaw, was costly for him. His next move was to the Doctor's office for treatment. The young lady was highly displeased with both men. She told them individually "Get out of my life." They did.

12

Bart O'Kelly was another of the many homesteaders in the area at that time. His homestead, consisting of one hundred sixty acres, was adjacent to his mother's home. Mother, Mary O'Kelly, kept a watchful eye over her only son. Bart, when asked, "Do you believe you'll ever get married?" His words were extemporaneously spoken. The response was, "Hell no!" No damn woman is never, ever going to tell me what to do!" A vivacious lady from Boston Massachusetts, arrived in Silver Lake. Her name was Pearl Oberholzer. Her eyes shone brighter than the brightest star in the heavens. Those eyes were focused on Bart. He soon succumbed to her advances. After a brief courtship, they became man and wife. During the early days of that whirlwind marriage, Pearl became more intolerant of the small cabin and the surrounding environment. She very emphatically and without any trepidation was domineering her new husband. Wing cigarettes were ten cents a pack. Bull Durham, roll your own cigarettes, was five cents for a small bag of tobacco. The small bag had sufficient paper to roll your own for approximately twenty cigarettes. Bart preferred the wing brand, thereby eliminating the time consuming, self made ones. Pearl was controlling the purse strings soon after the marriage vows were taken. She was less than generous when Bart asked for ten cents to buy a pack of smokes. Her tolerance was definitely limited when smokers were around. She would remove a quarter from her handbag; and hand it to Bart for his ten cent purchase with the stipulation that he return the unused fifteen cents to her for safe keeping. He cooperated in each instance. Bart was no longer on his own. Pearl was in control. Their departure from Silver Lake was imminent. Their new home was back in Massachusetts; and he never returned to Oregon to live. His final resting place is in Boston, Massachusetts.

13

New comers to the community were many and varied. They too, believed the railroad was coming to Silver Lake. Fred and Sally Adams had found a new home in Silver Lake. They brought Fred's nephew, Bruce Gaunt with them. Fred Adams was a barber. The couple had no available transportation. They lived within walking distance to town. The new barber in town located a vacant one room building for his hair cutting business. He barbered each Saturday, only. Each Saturday morning Fred, with a bed sheet filled with towels slung over his left shoulder, could be seen walking to town. In his right hand he carried a Coleman gasoline lantern and additional fuel. Additional fuel was required for the long Saturday hair cutting events. Adams was a good barber. His gestures were far above most barbers. Whenever a joke was told by a customer in the chair or a waiting customer, Fred had a better joke. His scissors rose far above his head and were clipping thin air when he told a better joke. Haircuts were twenty-five cents. Sally, had an idea to supplement their modest income. Her idea was to purchase a few silver foxes, ready them for the fur, skin and sell the furs to processors. Food for the animals, when purchased elsewhere was expensive. Jack rabbits were plentiful. Sally, with her twenty two rifle had the only answer. With her loaded rifle and her sharp eye leveled through the sights, she seldom missed a rabbit. She was called, "Dead Eyed Sally." They skinned the dead rabbits and flung the carcasses over the fence where the foxes were waiting for their dinner. The furry animals proved to be more lucrative than the barber chair.

Nephew, Bruce Gaunt, had a saddle horse and a pack mule. Gaunt lived alone, times were tough and Bruce was desperate for a job. His food was running low. Early one morning, he flung a pack saddle on the mule. He saddled his horse and headed to Hager Mountain in search of a deer to supplement his dwindling food supply. Bruce was also a "Dead Eye" through the sights of his thirty—thirty Remington rifle. The dividends were overwhelming. Ah Ha! he bagged one with the first shot. His next move, after disemboweling the dead animal was to lash his prize atop the pack mule. When he placed the dead animal on the pack mule, the mule became excited, spun around, and wrenched the halter rope from Bruce's extremely cold hands. The mule headed home carrying the well tied down dead animal on his back. Bruce quickly mounted his steed. The mule was moving fast, much too fast for the horse and rider. The mule, well ahead, arrived in the streets of Silver Lake for everyone to see. Fortunately for Bruce, a neighbor saw Bruce's pack mule with the deer's head dangling near the ground. A kind hearted neighbor moved the pack animal and deer into Mrs. O'Keefe's barn. Bruce gave the neighbor a hind quarter of the poached animal and no one talked. Bruce Gaunt was home free. The game warden was out of town.

14

Saturday nights much activity aroused the populace. Lucky Strike, Camel and Chesterfield cigarettes were 15 cents a pack. Not to be forgotten was home brew beer if available, ten cents a glass and moonshine from a local still. A still, through a heating process, is an apparatus used for distilling alcoholic beverages. Fermented mash from rye, wheat, corn or barley produced the desired taste. Many who became "well oiled" from the above mentioned beverages had sufficient leverage, they assumed, to proceed to the Odd Fellows Hall. The hall was where Saturday night dances were held. The home spun orchestra consisted of three musicians. Emil Egli played the violin, Chet Hollinshead thumped the drums, and several different ladies pounded the piano keys at different times and on different occasions. A young man in the community arrived late at a Saturday night dance wearing bright red pants. Ruffians took him to the woodshed, removed those pants, left him in the shed and locked him in that darkened, dingy hole. The perpetrators then took his pants and two brooms and reentered the dance hall. The pants were held high above the dance floor; with the two brooms placed inside and held in a vertical position. The marching began for everyone to see. Many were saddened by such unsolicited behavior. Bright red pants in that hall were never again displayed at that particular location.

15

Wheat from the Hunter Ranch in Summer Lake, was transported to Lone Pine Ranch. The wheat was used to fatten the now grown hogs. On Thanksgiving Day each year the hogs were butchered. Scalding vats containing hot water and wood ashes, when heated to the desired temperature, would loosen the hog hair. Butcher knives, used at right angle to the carcass, removed the hair. The hairless hog was disemboweled and hung head down for overnight cooling. The following day the head, shoulders, hams, sides used for bacon, and feet were beginning the long process of curing. Trimmings from the carcass were used for sausage. Particles from the carcass and around each piece were ground in a sausage grinder. Patties were formed from the ground pork which had been seasoned and cooked. The patties were packed in one half gallon jars. Hot lard made from fat was poured over the patties; and the jars were sealed with lids. Result "Yummy sausages" for the long hard winter.

The long laborious curing process was to salt and resalt. The pork was placed on a table and salted. The hams were the most difficult. To be successful, a pointed hardwood stick was inserted into the inner most part of the ham. After several days, the salt was removed from the meat and the hole in the ham. New salt was put on the meat and the open hole was filled with new salt. The next operation was to properly smoke each part. Smoke houses were plentiful during those times. Each piece was hung high above green willow or other greenery to suit your taste. The greenery, with a very small wood fire would be sufficient. Close the door and "let it smoke." This operation would be repeated over and over many times. Every spring Mother bought one hundred day old leghorn chickens. Roosters were for food and the hens were to supply eggs. Maurice, age six, was to be the one to drive a team of horses to move the fresh cut hay from the field to the hay stack over a slide. The repeated loads of hay would pile the hay higher and higher until the haystack was rounded off by the stacking crew with pitch forks. The hay stacks were thirty foot high. The greenhead flies were numerous and bothered the horses tremendously. Maurice had problems. The horses would shake their heads constantly, tangling the lines. Maurice had to call for help to untangle the lines time and time again. Hay was plentiful, pasture was adequate and the cattle herd was growing. The Emery's had purchased the Lone Pine Ranch in 1921 after having rented it for two years.

16

In 1923, it was time for Maurice's schooling to begin. The model T Ford and the nine miles to school would have been difficult. School busses were not available. The decision was made to have him stay five days a week with his grandparents, Elmer and Hema Graves, who lived one quarter mile from the school in Silver Lake. He could walk the short distance to and from the schoolhouse.

Silver Lake School

First grade 1923, Doris Gould, teacher

His first teacher was Doris Gould. This was her first teaching contract, after graduating from college. His next teacher was Mrs. Whelan. Mrs. Whelan taught the second and third grades for several years. Her husband, Edward, was the school caretaker. Mrs. Whelan was an extremely talented improvvisatore. Her improvisations and charm excited the children, as well as all the adults, who listened. Mr. Whelan stoked the furnace early each morning with wood cut in three foot lengths. Wood from nearby Hager Mountain was cut, split, hauled and stacked at a cost of three dollars and fifty cents a cord. Fifty cords a year were used to steam heat eight rooms including the library and auditorium. The gymnasium wasn't heated at that time, because of restrictions from a fire insurance standpoint. Later years, however, wood burning stoves were installed and extreme care was necessary in order to keep the structure safe.

La Pine school, smaller in size, had fewer students and therefore was less competitive. They, after being defeated repeatedly, decided, if they were unable to win in basket ball, they would win in another way. They sent eight husky lumber jacks to manually whip Silver Lake. The eight husky lumberjacks sat side by side on a bench. The cowboys were also tough hombres. The game was over, Silver Lake won. Fortunately, no bare knuckles were thrown and everyone went home peacefully. The high degree of animosity between the two rivals was brought to an abrupt end.

The 1921 Ford wasn't the most aggressive mode of transportation when climbing a mountain. The gasoline tank was located under the front seat. If you approached a steep incline, and the gas tank was less than half full; the engine would stop. It was necessary to back up the mountain in order for the fuel, gravity fed to the carburetor, to reach its final destination before entering the explosion chambers. When you reached the top of the incline, you would turn around and go forward again to reach your destination. Henry Ford had foresight. He believed in mass production of a vehicle that would (following the invention of the wheel) put the general public in a more comfortable mode of transportation. This would eliminate the droppings, odors and care needed for an animal drawn wagon or buggy. The Ford was an updated travel vehicle. Grandma, along side of Grandpa during their courting days, was thrilled. No odors, no harnessing a horse and less care. The rubber tires were also more quiet then iron wheels crunching the gravel roads before reaching their destination. Henry Ford was the first automobile manufacturer to pay five dollars a day to his employees.

Needless to say, the Ford had many discomforting ways. Connecting rod bearings would disintegrate leaving a loud knock coming from the engine. The touring public was aware of these sounds and many would carry a supply of bacon rinds. When they heard the problem, they would park along side the road, grab a few wrenches and crawl under the car and remove the oil pan. Next they would dismantle the connecting rod and wrap bacon rind around the crankshaft, retighten the connecting rod and replace the oil pan Down the road, much slower, would get you to a mechanic who could supply the part and take care of the installation. Cold weather and the Ford were much less than compatible. The custom was during freezing weather, to park the stubborn one under cover, build a small kindling fire under the engine and differential to warm the oil and grease. Jack up one rear wheel, and leave stubborn ford in gear. The jacked up wheel served as a balance while cranking. Battery operated ignitions were not yet available. July fourth, each year, farmers and ranchers would repaint the old vehicle, display two American flags installed on top of the windshield and have a community picnic. These occasions were held on Bridge Creek or Silver Creek year after year.

Slivers said "Boys, We will soon have a high powered car." A motorist walked to the ranch. His Star automobile had stopped running. Slivers traded him a team of horses, harness and buggy for the broken down vehicle. That was our "high powered car." Repairs to the Star car were finally completed Three small boys, covered with blankets, slept in comfort in the car parked in front of the Odd Fellows Hall; while their parents danced until the wee hours and the band stopped playing. The dance hall floor covered approximately six thousand square feet; and was used for other events such as movies which came to town infrequently.

17

The winter of 1924–1925 was bitterly cold. The temperature dropped to forty-eight degrees below zero. Those temperatures never rose above forty degrees below zero, day and night, for a consecutive ten day period. Ears and tails were frozen and later dropped off the animals. A one hundred fifty pound calf was frozen to death while standing. Nail heads around the door and window casings inside the house had protruding frost extending one-half inch into the room. Cold, in that part of the country, was never known to previously exist, nor has the cold been that severe since that 1924–1925 winter.

Everett "Slivers" Emery and Clarence "Link" Woodard formed a partnership aiming to build full fledged cattle producing empire. They purchased the Sullivan Ranch at Wagontire, Oregon. Woodard was to be in charge of the newly purchased ranch. Link Woodard, a single man, became involved with Link Hutton's wife. Hutton was about to seek revenge. Early one morning, at daybreak, another neighbor, Harold Bradley, appeared at the irritated neighbor's home. Believing Bradley was his competitor, he leveled his thirty-thirty rifle and shot and killed him. The murder prompted Woodard and the angry husband's wife to depart the area. Thirty years passed and no one knew the whereabouts of Woodard during his absence. This writer met a lady, at a bridge party in Wickenburg. Arizona, who lived in Blythe, California, the same time that Mr. Woodard lived there. She said that Mr. Woodard had bought an alfalfa farm and had prospered. She said that he was never called Link in that community. Wonder why not? Many years after Woodard's departure from Wagontire; and the shooting husband was dead, Mr. Woodard moved from Blythe to Mt Shasta, California, and retired from his alfalfa fields. He called Slivers who was also aged in years. They became once again best of friends enjoying each other's company. Slivers, years earlier, had sold the Wagontire spread to Frank Dobkins. Mr. Dobkins and Ira Bradley were shot and killed over cattle watering rights. One Suspect! No convictions!

18

Many rodeo fans, cowboys and those living there, believed Silver Lake could, with substantial effort, be a well known rodeo town. Several rodeos were well patronized. However, in the end, failures outweighed the desired results. Cecil Owsley and Doris "Pudd" Porter, disappointed as they were, decided to try something different. One evening they walked into a pool hall and fired a few shots from their revolvers into the ceiling. Jeff Howard, the proprietor, came forward from his poker game in the rear of the building and reminded both of them to desist such bad behavior. They then fired a couple more shots into the ceiling. Mr. Howard calmly took his revolver from a drawer behind the bar and fired. The bullet went through Porter's shirt, narrowly missing his arm. One of the outlaws then fired at Mr. Howard hitting him in the jaw. The aroused poker players came forward and lifted Mr. Howard, bleeding from the mouth, onto a nearby pool table. A doctor was summoned and Mr. Howard's beard was shaved from his face. The wound was not as serious as originally believed. The gun slingers were subsequently released from the "Pokey." Mr. Owsley was working as a hired hand at Lone Pine when he was involved in the shooting in the pool hall. His presence in that pool hall was not seen for some time, if ever. He and Slivers played checkers at the ranch during evening hours; thereby eliminating his desire to shoot holes in the ceilings of a pool hall. Cecil had schooled at Oregon State College and participated heavily in the sports classes. He was one of the best wrestlers around during those times. A huge Irishman, named Dan Horrigan, lived in the community. Dan was fearful of no one. His size, six foot six, weight at about two hundred forty pounds and his strength was unbelievable. Harassment on many occasions perturbed most of the populace, especially around the local pool hall. When asked, he would angrily shout "I can beat any man in town." When asked "Would you get in the ring with Cecil Owsley during the next rodeo?" He snorted "You damn well know, I would." The ring was assembled. Unbeknown to Horrigan, however, was the fact that Qwsley was an untiring, almost professional wrestler. Owsley knew if Horrigan got hold of him, he would squeeze the innards out of him. The match was about to begin. Owsley bounced from his corner, knocked Horrigan's feet aside, rolled him over and began the pummeling process. Owsley had Horrigan's legs twisted in a position that looked like a giant pretzel. Horrigan's long arms resembled a giant octopus reaching for his prey. He couldn't reach Owsley, however. Horrigan had been defeated at last!

19

The cattle herd was growing at the Lone Pine. Insufficient summer pasture posed a problem, if the herd was to be increased. Slivers rented the Loosley fields at Klamath Marsh for one year. During the summer, we camped at the corrals with bedrolls and grub box. There was no shelter from the elements. The White Ranch, nearby, was for sale in 1927. Sealed bids were used. Slivers was the lucky bidder. They, now had summer pasture; and everyone was more enthusiastic about the cattle baron possibilities. August 22, 1927, Maurice and Dale, with assistance from their parents, recorded the former Frank Bass branding iron, with the State of Oregon. They, at a very young age were looking forward to becoming enriched in the livestock industry. They believed prosperity was just around the corner. A few young calves were being branded with the boys' branding iron. A proper thing to do, according to the parents. The boys were working much harder now, anticipating a really bright future.

The summer was over and haystacks had been properly fenced at Lone Pine. It was time to take a day or two to visit neighbors and go to town. Maurice and Jack Shanahan were sitting on a bench together in town, when Jack said "Kid," always have a dollar in your pocket." He was obviously saying, if you have money, you'll be in a unique position to grab a bargain whenever one comes along. Good Idea! Once again, it was almost time to think about school. English teachers, in those days were high caliber professionals. Teachers were very emphatic, especially during English classes. They taught proper grammar throughout their tenure. Students dare not ever commence a sentence with the word "And." You were taught never to end a sentence with the word "At." Should you do so, a very stern, disgusting look from the teacher, would change your mind. You would be severely reprimanded.

The homestead house was moved to Silver Lake in 1924. Esther and the boys were to live at that location five days a week while attending school. George and Josephine Emery, the boys' grandparents, lived nearby the reconstructed homestead house. George and Josephine Emery had moved to town for the winters in order that their sons, Frank, Bill and Wayne could go to school. Josephine invited Maurice and Dale to live with them five days a week so they could go to school. Josephine now had five boys to keep in school five days every week. Maurice and Dale lived five days a week with their grandmother during school for two years. The reconstructed homestead house was rented to Bill "Sank" Howard, proprietor of the Pastime pool hall for five dollars a month

The weekends were a time for work at the ranch. Maurice and Dale gathered wood for the winters ahead. Two horse drawn wagons, log chains, axes, lunch and other equipment were aboard. The six mile, one way trip to Table Mountain was their destination. Arriving at the Mountain, they unhitched their horses from the wagon. Log chains were attached to the very top of the dead juniper trees. Horses, driven by the brothers, pulled down the trees. The next operation was to remove the limbs from the trees with their axes. The trees, many two feet in diameter, were rolled onto the wagons; and the six miles back to Lone Pine over a hot, dusty road was accomplished. The trees were split with wedges, axes, and sledgehammers into suitable size for the buzz saw. Power to run the saw, was derived from a jacked up rear wheel of the Model T Ford. A belt was used between the twelve inch pulley attached to the rear wheel; and the sounds of the juniper wood pushed through the saw sounded like two tom cats fighting on top of a wooden picket fence.

Homeward bound from Table Mountain with firewood.

20

Approximately thirteen years into this story, a tragic and deadly incident occurred. Mr. Trickey, riding in an open vehicle at an annual Lakeview Roundup Parade was sitting beside a lady companion Mrs. Trickey disliked very much. Mrs. Trickey, an onlooker with a knife, was ready for the open air vehicle to pass by. She, with knife in hand, jumped on the running board and thrust the knife into the heart of Mr. Trickey. That was a disaster that most onlookers had never seen before!

Adin McCall and Slivers Emery, from Silver Lake were seated as jurors. Lorena Trickey had committed a crime. Her lawyers were extremely competent and their expletives brought tears to the eyes of several jurors. Mrs. Trickey was acquitted of a horrendous crime!

21

The 1929 stock market crash would soon be a devastating, intolerant, horrible blow to many millions of Americans. Fred Reynolds, president of the Bank of Lakeview, called on Slivers to take and run a band of sheep. Slivers said "I am a cowman! I don't herd sheep!" However, Slivers lost that battle. That was prior to the Taylor Grazing Act. Now, the Lone Pine was running both cattle and sheep. The sheep were grazed mostly on public land. Two years passed and Reynolds selected Granville Hardisty of Lakeview, as the new sheep keeper, with the provision that Slivers send along a man to help out temporarily. Maurice, age sixteen, and Adin McCall were Hardisty's hired help.

Hardisty was a good boss. He was a musician and played a violin. He never exhibited his musical ability to his hired men. His sheet music and violin were not compatible with the sheep business. Our listening to his musical ability was not his choice. Occasionally, we would catch him unaware that anyone was around and we would listen. His music was highly accepted, especially by those with limited musical talent. Young lambs, ewes and wethers were corralled for "docking." Maurice was in the midst of the operation. His job was to remove the testicles from the male sheep with his teeth. This job is presently done with hand held clamps. After the first five hundred that day, a bloody face and clothing seemed to be the only problem. He continued on and completed the operation on a thousand more wethers. The sheep were shorn, wool sold and delivered. We were now ready to trail the band to summer range. Mr. Hardisty had a Model A Ford pickup. He told Adin that he would be our camp tender.

The long trek to Quarts Mountain would take about one week. Quarts Mountain is between Bly and Lakeview. Burros were a necessity in most sheep bands. We had a burro to carry incidentals and bed rolls while on the range for short periods of time. Adin wasn't sure Hardisty would be with us all the way. He remarked: "I think we should pack the burro." Sure enough, the boss caught up with us one day before our arrival at Quarts Mountain six days later. Hardisty paid the necessary wages I had earned.

22

The belief was, while Slivers was traveling from Klamath Marsh to Lone Pine, he caught an aroma from one of the distilleries in Bear Flat or Antelope Flat. His downward spiral was imminent. Maurice took his hard earned wages and enrolled in the Adcox Diesel and Automotive School in Portland, Oregon. Room and board was twenty dollars a month. He walked one half mile to catch the trolley car to downtown Portland. The fare was five cents, "Girly "shows were ten cents. After the shows, near the Willamette River water front, coffee and two donuts cost ten cents. One young man, from Salt Lake City, had a Model A Ford. The Ford, with a rumble seat, would take five passengers. Contributions of up to one dollar for gasoline provided leisure trips around the city. Maurice ran out of money; and could no longer afford to pay room and board. Hard times were really here!.

Maurice returned to Lone Pine. When the dust bowl began, there was no cattle feed, neither hay nor grass was available. Grasshoppers invaded Klamath Marsh. Poisoning the hoppers was a never ending job. Afternoon and evening was spent mixing sawdust, bran, arsenic poison, molasses and banana oil flavoring to poison the pesky, hungry, flying, leaping insects. At day break the next morning, if possible, you would challenge the pests. The poison was loaded onto horse drawn wagons and was thrown, by hand, onto the many, many beds of newly hatched devourers of cattle pasture. The ranchers in the area gathered at the Military Crossing to plan a strategy to rid the area of the powerful hind leg jumping creatures. Walter Kittredge, brother of Bill Kittredge, was among the group. The sky was darkened by the hungry pests. Walter Kittredge dismounted and threw his bridle reins into a cluster of the pests and shouted. "The son's o bitches!" Two families from Denver, Colorado, subsequently arrived with five thousand six-week old turkeys. The idea was good. Turkeys were going to have a real grasshopper feast before being taken to Klamath Falls for grain fattening. The turkeys, as they became older, would focus their attention on a hopper. The flying hoppers excited the turkeys. Chasing the hoppers sent the turkeys in many different directions and out of control. Housewives, fanning turkeys with their kitchen aprons, were unable to control the flock. Maurice, much to his disgust, was now going from sheepherder to a turkey herder with a saddle horse. He was hired for one dollar a day to help herd turkeys. Ten days later, the turkeys that were captured, were shipped to the fattening pens. Maurice didn't get his ten dollars. The turkey people were out of money. He did get his money later when the turkeys were sold.

23

The dust bowl era was upon most of the country west of the Mississippi River. A few areas of Klamath County were blessed with grasses and hay. Klamath Marsh was one. Hundreds of cattle in the Midwest part of the country were dying of starvation. Klamath County Indians, with cattle feed at that time, could buy starving registered herefords for one dollar a head. The bovines arrived in railroad stock cars. Some had died in those cars. The dead ones were removed. The others were skin and bones. George Duvall and Indian Wife accepted their allotment. George hired Knerr "Kob" Buick to help. Wild hay was stacked for the winter. This hay was not of the best quality. Many of George's herd did not survive the following winter. Harsh winters, in that part of the country, during long winter months, are bitterly cold, windy and desolate. The one room log cabin was a haven for George and Kob. Dead cattle carcasses were numerous the following spring. Winter cattle feed at Lone Pine was non-existent for several years. Cattle were driven to the Sid Harris ranch in Summer Lake. Hay was purchased from the Harris Ranch and daily feeding was necessary. The daily trip, in a 1930 Ford coup, was, at times, exhausting.

The Thousand Springs Ranch, on the east side of Summer Lake, once owned by L. D. Hoy, was rented for a number of years. Grassy meadows were irrigated, mowed, raked and stacked exclusively by the Lone Pine crews. Alkali, sand dunes and sulfur water are well known at this location. We would, when hauling haying equipment to this ranch, first remove the sulfur water from the underground domestic supply. The standing water, not being used daily, had a sulfur smell and a sulfur taste. After the long, unused spring was bailed out, the taste was more tolerant. The house was a seven room. single story L shaped one; and had sufficient room for the hay crew. Modern showers were not available at that time. The Hoys, before their departure, left abandoned cream separator parts on the premises. The used bowls were placed over head. Temporary structures beneath the bowls, dimensionally suitable for one hay hand at a time to take a shower. Below the spigot, a tin can with a series of small holes was attached thereto. Under the tin can, reaching upward you would open the spigot for a very refreshing shower. After showers were taken, the bowl was replenished with cold, sulfur water. The summer sun, the followday, would warm the water for the next occupant.

Jim Foster, grandson of the Hoys; and wife, Teressa own and occupy the ranch. Daughter, Elizabeth and family live nearby on the former Bonham Ranch. It is extremely difficult to properly assess the serenity of the Thousand Springs Ranch. The Foster lineage will, hopefully, continue on, in a traditional manner. Teressa Foster, author of Settlers In Summer Lake Valley, should be congratulated for her time and effort necessary to write and edit an outstanding publication.

Brother Kenneth was not much help during the haying seasons. He was more interested in hunting and trapping.

Kenneth with gun in hard headed to his hunting grounds in 1935

However, he changed dramatically when he reached the age of seventeen. He abused his body in many ways. He was thrown from horses on to rock piles, wrangled cattle, and over worked his body in many ways. Hard work was his choice. His enthusiasm for ranch style living, never faltered. Brother Dale's patience for Kenneth's actions was limited, however. Maurice, in the meantime, unbeknown to the rest of the family, was saving his hard earned dollars. Having attended Adcox School the previous year and having insufficient funds for college, he became more interested in business schools. One summer he stacked alfalfa hay for his grandfather Graves, thereby "stacking" away a few more dollars. The Lone Pine Ranch, at that time, became less interesting to me due to hard times. I once again, enrolled in school at Oregon Institute of Technology in Portland, Oregon. The school, at that time, was located at 15th and Taylor streets in Portland. Aircraft structures, and welding were among the most interesting. The home away from home was, again, in a three story boarding house located where the Lloyds Center is presently located. I studied diligently; but ran out of money before the courses were finished. Returning to Silver Lake, I was once again on home turf.

Several events occurred during my absence. The Chewaucan Land and Cattle Company, based in Paisley, Oregon, had an employee, named Napitan. The company also had a cattle ranch two miles west of Silver Lake at the mouth of Bridge Creek. The company hired many new ranch hands to pitch hay from the haystacks onto wagons to feed the cattle. Mr. Napitan and a newly hired ranch hand, one frosty morning, were loading a wagon. Unbeknown to the new employee, Napitan was a prankster of sorts. Napitan planted an unusually large pile of hay at the base of the fully loaded wagon. He summoned the new employee to help lift the hay to the top of the load. After several attempts, the hay was still "fastened to the ground." Napitan said, "We'll try one more time; and if we aren't successful, you take your fork out." The new employee was completely unaware that Napitan was pushing his fork downward each time they tried. The new man on the job removed his fork; and, low and behold, the hay landed immediately on top of the load due to the dexterity of Napitan.

24

The early nineteen thirties were especially uneventful, but they were occasionally humorous. A loving couple were to be married on a certain date at a local Baptist Church. The lovers were in complete agreement on the specified date. Their friends and neighbors were thrilled immeasurably. The groom wasn't considered the most reliable person in the community. His father gave him sufficient spending money; some of which was used to purchase a new Ford automobile. Poker games at the Pastime Pool Hall were his choice of entertainment. He would drive and park the new car near the pool hall, leave the driver's door wide open and go into the pool hall for his usual games of poker. There were those who took advantage and drove around the country side until the gas tank was nearly empty. They would return the vehicle to the same location where it had been parked, leaving it with the driver's door open and the key in the ignition with the engine running. Many times the fuel was burned away while the car stood idling. The owner, not being aware he had departed the vehicle in a drive away condition, called for help. Gasoline was replenished and he would drive away completely unaware that joy riders had traversed the countryside.

Now, it was time for the wedding at the church. The bride arrived on schedule. The well-wishers were comfortably seated in their respective pews. The minister was ready to perform his duty. The groom was not forthcoming. Two hours passed and no groom. Tense minutes prevailed. The crowd dispersed. Three days passed. Still no Groom! The fourth day the groom reappeared. Well wishers and the nervous couple, on the fourth day after the original scheduled ceremony was abandoned, came forward. The church was overflowing with friends and well wishers. The minister and the wedding ring united the obstreperous man and his lovely bride. What a wedding!

Witnesses to the harmonious event were mobilized for a traditional shivaree. The couple departed the church, hand in hand, and approached their get away car. Rice and beans were thrown. The ground was covered with both. They were well on their way to parts unknown. The newly-weds well knew pranksters and fun lovers would probably follow. The couple took off at a high rate of speed. The cloud of dust was over whelming behind the newly married couple. However, the dust failed to deter the many cars chasing after the couple. Midway between Silver Lake and Fort Rock the lead car, carrying a sharpshooter with a loaded gun, closed in on the fleeing vehicle. The sharpshooter took aim at a rear tire. His first shot was successful in a big way. The tire was flattened. Well wishers surrounded the worried honeymoon escapees. They installed the spare tire for the newly weds The happy couple continued on their journey grateful that a flat tire was the worst thing that happened to them. The shivareers returned to their respective homes. Clyde, Jot and Tom Nelson were single brothers who lived together on the S O Ranch. Moonshine from the ranch appeared at many social events. Where did they acquire the beverage? Many were suspicious. No one knew. Clyde was, he assumed, to be a clear-cut ladies' man; and was ignored by most women, if not all women.

25

School was in session. Roy Sawyer was the principal. Sawyer was small in stature, very capable and extremely confident of his position as the school's head master. The solid stone, eight room building housed grades one through twelve. Approximately one hundred students and five teachers were involved. One very strict teacher never allowed students to move from their desks unless they were given permission to do so.

A third grade student, Bob Sinclaire had "itchy britches" and would purposely break the lead of his pencil during classes. He would raise his hand to seek permission to return to the pencil sharpener. The teacher had previous knowledge of his uncontrollable behavior. She would ask "Bob, why did you break your pencil again?" He would respond. "It broke by itself!" Her answer was "Now, you will fail this assignment" Bob had the answer. He immediately gnawed his teeth around the broken end and began a bitter chewing process. Distasteful as it was, this chewing procedure ultimately trimmed the wood from the lead. The lead was not well rounded, however. Bob finished the writing assignment with a blunt pencil, never, again, asking permission to trot over to the pencil sharpener.

Prior to modern plumbing facilities, we had open pit out houses. Two buildings, one for the boys and one for the girls. These "places for comfort" were buildings twelve by twelve foot square. Nothing comparable to today's comfort stations. Odors were abhorrent The girls walking single file, hand in hand, or in groups marched from the school house to these "discomforting" comfort stations. The girls entries to the out houses were especially attractive to the boys hiding behind the sagebrushes nearby. Boys, with a hand full of rocks, crouched behind a sagebrush, were ready to fling their salvos of rocks at the white painted building with the girls seated inside. Screams and cries came from within. Mr. Sawyer, once appeared near the scene. All boys were severely reprimanded. No more "rocking the girls," while entrapped as they sat in an uncomfortable comfort station.

Located behind the gymnasium, was a baseball field. Along side the gym was where the boys played marbles. Girls were excluded from these areas. Jim Cliff, at bat, swung hard. The ball and bat made a perfect connection. Soaring through the air, out of the ball field and across the street, it was much more than a home run. Unfortunately the ball shattered Mr. and Mrs. Pitchers' plate glass window and landed in their living room. They were not at home. It is assumed that the Pitchers paid for the window to be replaced.

26

Store bought toys and expensive Christmas presents for the next few decades were non existent. Christmas presents consisted of home made clothes and various toys constructed of wood by parents. Children, many times, were fortunate if they found a monkey on a string, a mouth harp, small bits of candy and a few oranges. Tiddly winks and the above mentioned toys would demoralize most modern day children. Tiddly winks needs further clarification by an old fogy. Here's how it is played. It is a game in which the players try to snap small colored disks from the floor or table into a cup by pressing the edges of the colored disks with a larger disk. "Monkey on a String" was a small monkey approximately six inches long with a small cord affixed to a nail or similar object on the wall. The cord, when doubled, hanging toward the floor, was inserted in the small monkey's head. The two cords came out near the monkey's rear end. The monkey was now on the string. When one end of the cords was pulled from the bottom, the monkey would climb upwards. The other end, hanging down, when pulled, would lower the monkey for yet another round of entertainment. That was called, "Children's-Monkey-Business."

27

George and Patricia Wall homesteaded ten miles from Silver Lake. The one hundred and sixty acres was their pride and joy. Their house was a typical one, constructed with the usual board and bat frame style. Water was carried from a nearby neighbor's hand dug well in five gallon milk cans. The unsophisticated and many times contaminated water was abhorrent and distasteful when swallowed. Moreover, the smell was obnoxious. Wooden framework covering the hand dug wells in those days were not sufficiently constructed to keep mice and other rodents from entering and falling into the water below. The result was nasty water. A rope tied to a bucket was used to hoist the water and contaminants to the surface, empty the mess and repeat the process, when the water, once again, became safe for use.

Patricia had an idea, she said, "George, we are going to dig our own well!" George replied, "Pat, we don't have the strength to do that!" Pat countered, "Why not?" George replied, "We are too old; and do not know how to dig a well!" Pat had another idea. She drove her old car to town. George was home alone with Fluffy, the cat. When Pat returned, she had the necessary tools and equipment to try and convince George to undertake the horrendous task ahead. Her tools consisted of a one inch hemp rope, a heavy five gallon bucket, a miner's rock pick, a short handled shovel and a windlass that she borrowed from a neighbor on her return to the homestead. George was unhappy while observing her newly purchased well digging equipment. Neither slept well that night. They rolled and tossed. Their feelings toward each other was less than normal. Fried rabbit and hotcakes were forced down at the breakfast table. Pat exited the house, grabbed the shovel and reentered, handing George the handle. George retorted "Did you buy a pair of gloves while in town?" She reached into a back pocket, pulled them out and said "Yes, I did. Try them on!" New gloves George's size felt better than anticipated. Tensions lessened. A sight was selected near the back door for a new well. Pat began with a few shovels removed from the top of the starting point. George stood silently by, his hands in his pockets, completely bewildered. The windlass was not needed at this starting point. It was not set in motion as long as dirt could be thrown, conveniently out of the hole with the shovel.

At approximately seven feet deep, it was no longer feasible to throw the dirt out of the hole with the shovel. George, with his half worn out gloves and a hot shovel handle, climbed out. The windlass was placed over the well to be. A windlass is an apparatus operated by hand, for hauling or hoisting. It consisted of a drum or cylinder upon which is wound the rope which is attached to the object to be lifted. George's job was to fill the five gallon bucket with the newly dug dirt as he lowered himself deeper into that darkened hole. Pat, with her strong arms, had George "in the hole," for many days ahead. The exception was; time for lunch, dinner or bedtime. These exceptions were George's happiest times. He, standing flat footed in the bucket, his weary hands clutching the rope, was hoisted, time after time, into the sunshine above. Anything, other than dirt which George had to expel, was entered into the bucket, brought to the surface and placed far away in sun heated rocks or sagebrush.

After the eighteenth day, before breakfast, George wasn't feeling well. He demanded a day off from that pick and shovel job. Pat was concerned. She said, "No work today!" Alas, he felt relieved. He had two days off. Before returning to the, "hole in the ground," a slight disagreement occurred. Fluffy, the cat, slithered beneath George's feet. His number twelve shoe landed on top of the cat's tail. The cat yowled. The fight was on between Pat and George. Fluffy was Pat's cat. On the twenty-first day and twenty feet below the earth's surface, a few drops of water oozed from the dirt beneath his tired aching feet. Sighting a few drops of water made him thirsty. Peering from the bottom upward where Pat was standing, looking down, George, looking upward, called, "Pat, send me down a drink of water with the next bucket!" Pat roared, "Dig for it, you son of a bitch!" Those well digging ventures didn't prove to be successful. They are long gone. Drillers with modern equipment and expertise have solved the back breaking, antiquated, pick and shovel method. Clean, clear water is presently enjoyed by those living in that high desert country. George and Pat Wells left the arid area soon after that encounter with the earth.

28

An honorable man, Jim Wells, arrived in the community. He was no relation to George and Patricia. His previous knowledge was wide and varied. He was a brick layer by trade; and had worked previously in large metropolitan areas. Wells soon became aware of the red rock quarry at Bridge Creek near the Owsley Ranch. His enthusiasm for the unique treasure was overwhelming. The only tools he took to the site were a crowbar and a hand axe. He would sink the crowbar between the many layers; and pry them apart for further examination. He determined that the twelve inch wide layers were soft and easily squared with his axe. His first few swings with the axe proved successful. The soap-stone was easily manageable and could be used for construction purposes. Jim talked to several local residents regarding the possibilities for the construction of above ground cellars to be used during the extremely cold winters. The idea was to replace the underground cellars with a more convenient and accessible structure.

After working several days at the open pit mine, piles of lightweight, red rock were piled high for inspection. Local residents were amazed. Wells suggested that two walls be constructed three inches apart for temperature control. The two walls would be warm in winter time and cool during the summer months. The skillfully hewn, irregular lengths would be cemented together with a three inch "dead space," between the two walls. E. J. Egli, garage and service station proprietor, was number one on the list for Well's idea. The stone was loaded on horse drawn wagons and transported to the building site. Days later the building was completed with a wooden roof and a six inch thick wooden door. Between the rooftop and the ceiling inside, multiple layers of sawdust were evenly placed. The six inch thick entry door was also packed with sawdust. Wife, Verna Egli, was extremely impressed with her newly constructed storage room. The owners of the Lone Pine Ranch were also impressed with the newly constructed storage facility. The second storage house was constructed at the Lone Pine Ranch. That storage house is presently abandoned. The original farm house that burned many years later was replaced by a new one in a different location. The Lone Pine Ranch and the E. J. Eglis' stock piled their food in glorified security from the bitter cold winter weather. Skaags Safeway Store in Bend was where most food supplies were purchased. It is not presently known if Skaggs was one of the original investors or if the name Skaggs was **a** fictitious name. The name was changed. Safeway is presently a national food store chain. Those born after the name change will be doubtful. However it's true.

29

Mr. Wells had other interests in the Community, as well. His propensities exceeded his opportunities. His many admirers asked him if he had experience in age-old ice storage. His reply was, "Not much." Henry Egli and crew invited Jim to accompany them to Silver Creek; where two foot thick ice was to be garnered for the hot summer months ahead. Horses, wagons and drivers were ready. Ice saws, ice tongs and axes were loaded aboard. Axes were necessary to chop through the ice for the saws, hand operated, to begin the cutting process. The ice was marked in eighteen inch squares on the surface. Ice saws do not have a drag as required on wood saws. Wood saws require a drag to bring out the sawdust. Ice saws are constructed to take the shavings along with each stroke. An ice cube is buoyed by the water surrounding every ice cube. While the floating ice is being eyed by the crew, a man with the tongs grabs each chunk and slides it up a wooden plank onto the wagon. When the load is completed, the crew, in haste, heads for the ice house. The wagon master backs the wagon near the door. Once again, the many pieces of ice are placed on top of several inches of sawdust side by side. That is called, "snuggling." In each instance the mountain of ice is placed no closer than six inches from any outside wall. The six inch space is where more sawdust is packed tightly for preservation throughout the summer months. Ice packed with saw dust, as required, lasts several months. Ice cream, an entirely different process, required the attention of the fairer sex. Men have the ability to properly cool their Coors, Budweiser and Hams beer.

Jim Wells was an admirable man. His interests in the Community were gratefully accepted. His personal wealth, due to those depressing times, was undoubtedly minimal. Due to his inability to easily awaken when the sun arose, he headed for Klamath Falls in search of steady employment. A local man found him in Klamath Falls. He had a steady job at the Pelican Lumber Company. He stated that he had a good job and a nice comfortable apartment. He was concerned about his deep sleep syndrome. He needed the job. He further stated that he had purchased two new alarm clocks and two huge galvanized washtubs. He placed the washtubs upside down near his bed; and an alarm clock placed on top of each tub. Both alarms were set to ring at the same time. Should one fail to ring, the second one would awaken him. He figured this would insure that he would not be late for work again.

30

Lily Hoard, a well respected school teacher, came to Silver Lake in the late nineteen twenties. She taught fourth and fifth grades. Miss Hoard was born in St. Hilaire, Minnesota, November 10, 1895. Her tenure, at the school lasted for several years. Miss Hoard married Dean Hollinshead. The Hollinsheads' lived in Bend, Oregon, for the remainder of their lives. Dean died during the early 1980's. He was a hauling contractor, hauling mail and freight between Bend and Lakeview. His stage line, at one time, took passengers and mail as far away as Weed, California. Both were well known philanthropists. They bequeathed their horse ranch to the City of Bend previous to their demise. The Hollinsheads' were sponsors and avid supporters of the Rimrock Riders Association. Their horses were always well groomed. Their attire was outstanding. They and other riders were well known and equally respected. Mrs. Hollinshead was confined to a nursing home prior to her death July 23, 1990. She had no children. Two nieces were at her funeral. Indeed a saddening experience for the "one only" former student in attendance. She left behind a legacy that was, and is, hard to follow.

31

Three well known individuals who left Silver Lake and became foresters were Harold Carrick, Timothy Woods and George William (Bill) Emery. Bill and Dorothy Emery are believed to have commenced their forestry work at Bear Butte near Bear Flat, as "lookouts." Lookouts were, for many years, stationed high atop a mountain or a butte looking for smoke from a distance. Where there's smoke there's fire below. At the sight of smoke, their observations were communicated to firefighters nearby. The crew, when approaching the fire in haste, were ready to do battle until the fire was extinguished. Needless to say, these stations were primitive. Drinking water, food and incidentals were hand carried up the rough trails to the upper most point for a full day of observation. Lookout workers, when night time was approaching, would back track to their respective cabins or tents below. Accommodations were better below than being on top of the mountain. Early the following morning, they would begin their long trek to be, once again, on top looking for smoke. Approximately twenty miles from Bear Butte was another Butte with a similar observation point. Indians and whites both called this butte Hard Pecker Butte. It was commonly known as such. The United States Forest Service frowned on that traditionally designated name. Their opposition was opposed by Indians and ranchers alike. However, the foresters won. The butte was renamed Round Butte and their records reflect that it shall be called Round Butte. Locals continued to call it Hard Pecker Butte; and they still call it Hard Pecker Butte. Forester, Tim Wood's and Clarence Adams, painting contractor, lived near Reno, Nevada. There is no evidence that their paths ever crossed. Adams left the area previous to Wood's arrival in the community. Tim and Mrs. Woods arrived back in the area in nineteen ninety-seven. The Woods' had relocated in Bend after their long time of service with the Forest Service near Reno, Nevada.

32

Silver Lake School had many determined students. One young lady had three older brothers. Brothers do, many times, harass the smaller siblings. That was a well known fact. Gymnastic classes were held each day. Boys and girls were in these classes together. Every girl wore black bloomers from the waist to the knees. Maurice, in one of his mischievous moods, snapped Lena Freeman on the butt with a rubber band. Lena screamed in rage. She was five foot tall. Maurice was much taller than Lena, and much younger. The girls came running to find out what happened. Lena said to Maurice "If you don't behave yourself, I will take you down and pee in your eyes." Girls much bigger than Lena were willing to assist Lena. Then, there were also the three brothers who would certainly be happy to help. The prankster was scared, embarrassed and then cautious. He immediately left the area. Forty years later when he was six foot four; and Lena was still five foot, they met on the street in Bend, Oregon. They greeted each other and embraced. He was working in California and was visiting at the Lone Pine Ranch. Lena was a retired business woman. Both were glad to see each other. With a "wry smirk," he suggested maybe she would like to carry out her threat. She replied, "Ah, forget that incident, that happened so long ago." Time may come and time may go; but friendship goes on forever.

Bill LaSlater was the one and only forest ranger during the earlier days at the nearby ranger Station. The LaSlaters had only one child, Louise. During the winter months, when the snow was knee deep to a tall giraffe; Bill would chain up all four wheels on his Model T Ford. When asked, "Bill, why are chains on the front wheels?" His response was "To keep the car from slipping sideways" Good thinking, perhaps. LaSlater, with chains on all four wheels was now, ready to take daughter Louise to school, one mile from their home. He would stop as close to the main door, as possible. Louise was safely inside until four o'clock when her dad would return for her. The LaSlaters lived only a short time in the community. Clarence Young and wife replaced the LaSlaters. Mr. Young was, once again, the one and only forest ranger.

The Young's had three children, Albert, Dorothy and Helen. Albert was the older one. Dorothy and Helen were attractive to local, younger, next-in-line ranchers to be. Albert was very athletic; and was a good basket ball player. Without him on the team, Silver Lake would not have been the winners they were. Albert was also a forester. He lived in Klamath Falls and on many occasions purchased lottery tickets, anticipating a win. One ticket purchased proved him a winner. Couldn't happen to a better man. Dorothy became the wife of a well known Fort Klamath cattleman, Lloyd Nicholson. Her new name was Dorothy Nicholson. Helen was last seen, by this author, in 1933 or 1934 in Vancouver, Washington. She was working as a waitress. She was busy and our conversation was limited. Her married name is unknown. Her whereabouts is, likewise, unknown.

The Bradley girls. Leah, Iris and Grace were in school during those trying times. However, they were in different classes. Their older sisters, Lora, Lena and Ruth were not in attendance at the Silver Lake School at that time. Their older brothers, Hosmer and Harold had moved from the area. Leah married and lived in Florida the rest of her life, seldom returning to her birthplace. Iris Jones lived in Paisley and Portland. Her final years were in Lakeview. Grace married Emil Gowdy. the Gowdy's had two sons who are presently known as "Gowdy Brothers" Electrical Contractors. Their home base is in Redmond, Oregon. The brothers are one of the largest electrical contracting companies in the state of Oregon. Hosmer Bradley married Neva Graves. A son, Harold and a daughter, Leila were their children. The family lived in Mendota, California in 1939.

33

The Andrews family owned a grocery store in Silver Lake. The family of four were a happy foursome. Mother, Stella, was an exuberant lady. Her bright eyes were a pleasure to see. Most of those who departed the area will remember daughter, Molly. She was extremely competent and desirous of having a business of her own. She owned a bakery in Sweet Home, Oregon, for many years. She now wishes she could live forever. She too, returns to the High Country on many occasions, when convenient. Glen Buchannan and Forest Stratton lived near Klamath Falls. They both married. Glen lived several miles north of the city along Highway 97. Stratton lived several miles south of the city, also adjacent to the same highway. They too, are also gone from this earth. Brothers, Homer and Wendell Pitcher went north to Alaska. They purchased fishing boats and became very successful in the fishing business.

Allegra Feess was the seventh grade teacher. Son, Paul, and daughter, Ruth, attended the same classes under her tutorship. Paul, in one of his wiser moments, decided to make some spending money. He purchased a used Maytag gasoline powered engine and a well worn six volt generator. A vee belt connected the engine and generator together. The engine was filled with a gasoline and oil mixture. The oil was added for proper lubrication to the single cylinder engine. Paul was in business. He contacted every automobile owner who had batteries in their cars. He was unaware that battery powered radios were soon to be marketed for the general public. Radios soon appeared. He was overwhelmed. Possibilities excited him! He was also aware that radios needed six volt batteries. Batteries could not hold their power for more than about two weeks; when a radio was tuned in for the long evenings. He charged one dollar for his recharges. Excited he was! He had plenty of spending money.

The games of checkers, tiddly winks, cards and telling tall stories was no longer the only type of recreation. Those who had radios relaxed in their rocking chairs and listened to the radio. Previous to the wide spread purchases of the battery powered radios, the smaller children in the area, walked three miles to the T.C. "Cull" Hamilton Ranch. Mr. and Mrs. Hamilton had the first radio in Nineteen twenty five. Soon thereafter Leston and Anna Linebaugh had their number two adventure. Leston was the distributor and salesman for radios. He was also the deputy sheriff. His salesmanship capabilities out distanced many of the local residents. A fire, during the late twenties, burned the Linebaugh and Groth store to the ground. That was a terrible disruption The store had a huge walk-in safe where records were kept. Monies from previous sales were also kept there. The night of the fire the door to the safe was inadvertently left unlocked and open. The fire was devastating to the partners. All records were lost forever. Residents also mourned the loss. The following day, after the fire, there was nothing standing but the concrete safe-like vault. The door was open wide. Coins were burned beyond recognition. A small piece of nugget like gold was found. It was later determined that the nugget looking specimen was formerly a gold watch. With limited insurance settlements, the Linebaughs purchased Dr. Thom's residence. Dr. Thom was the one and only resident doctor ever in Silver Lake. His office fronted his home. The office was a two room one. The good doctor left his practice and moved away during the stressful times around 1925. Families were expanding rapidly. Newborns were "coming out" like guests at a happy hour. Parents were unable to pay the doctor for his services; and additional booming baby business. His new office was located on the second floor in the O'Kane building in downtown Bend. He was a good doctor. His impoverishment disappeared.

34

Mary Walker came to the community around 1932 as a newly hired school teacher. Her two sons, Kenneth and Bill, accompanied her. The sons were different in many ways. Bill was cool, confident and more reserved than his younger brother. Kenneth was more commonly known as Kenny during his earlier years in school. He was as curious as a cub bear looking for its first tree to climb. This great explorer was invited to the Lone Pine Ranch to witness a beef butchering process. The young animal was corralled and ready for the kill. Kenny stood silent during the entire process, he watched with unmitigated enthusiasm. The hide was removed. The lower legs and head were removed with a very sharp butcher knife. The belly was split down the middle for removal of all internal organs. The upper part of the hind legs were attached to an overhead hoist, which lifted the carcass upwards. On the way up, the entrails began falling out. Juices were also oozing toward the ground below. The liver placed upon a table nearby was to be eaten in the not too distant future. Kenny sliced off a few pieces for his mother and brother Bill. He wasn't sure he would partake. At the dinner table that evening, however, he did eat some liver. He enjoyed the taste especially after it had been garnished with onions. The following day at school, he quipped, "I think I will become a doctor!" In nineteen thirty-four he changed plans. He thought about the time required, to be a successful doctor and surgeon. He said, "I'd rather become a dentist."

Kenny enrolled in the North Pacific College in Portland, Oregon, immediately following his momentous decision. We lived on Northeast Sixth Street, three blocks apart. Both in low-cost boarding houses. Kenny in college and Maurice at Oregon Institute of Technology. We lived nearby our respective schools. One Friday evening, Kenny called and invited me to go to the college with him. Slightly suspicious, however, I accepted his invitation. Classes were not being held on Saturday morning. He had special privileges and a key to the uppermost floor which we were to ascend. Being fully aware of his many and varied antics, I was more suspicious. Six or eight vats approximately eight foot long and three wide were filled with a liquid and formaldehyde. The odor rising like a cloud from the vats was extremely obnoxious. The vats were about three foot deep and in perfect alignment. A braided wire protruded above the surface of the obnoxious fumes. The boisterous dentist, to be, grabbed a wire and dragged a beheaded man out of the tank onto a table. With sharp knives and various other instruments, he began a carving process. The heart and liver were removed. His sharp knife sliced the man's liver as had been done on the beef back at the ranch. When asked, "Kenny do dentists working on a person's teeth, have to go this far?" His immediate reply was, "Yes, they do!" I don't remember sleeping too well that night. Hopefully Kenny did. He graduated with flying colors and got his state approved license to practice, when tragedy struck. He was paralyzed as a result of Multiple Sclerosis. He never opened an office. His remaining years confined him to a wheel chair. He died at the age of sixty years. It is really disheartening to see a good man, "go down!"

35

The Iverson family relocated from Fresno, California, to Lake County in 1929. They were an energetic family. Anita Iverson Bannister was postmistress in Paisley, Oregon until her retirement. One incident in particular occurred during a robbery. It was frightening beyond belief. During a recent interview, Anita reiterated the story about the robbery. The robbers had weapons. Post office employees were, with guns to their heads, directed to lie face down on the floor. Scary moments followed. One robber left the post office on foot and headed north. His path was beneath the Summer Lake rim rocks paralleling the lake. Ranches and homes lined the shores. His path through the thick under brush hindered law enforcement officers for several days. His hunger and tired feet finally slowed him down. Officers, with high powered binoculars and sharp eyes, closed in. He was captured without a struggle. The post office employees, with heart beats once again nearing normal, were back at work.

Lily Hoard Hollinshead, school teacher, once stated. "I don't know what all these young people are going to do. How are they going to make a living?" Flea the area? They did! Example: Most relocated in California. One in Connecticut. One in Florida and one in Mississippi. Many in various other parts of Oregon. Some in Nevada, Idaho and Washington. Pearl Adams married Jesse Pennington. The Penningtons', happily married, raised a family on a ranch in Summer Lake. They were survivors in a community nearby.

36

The "Great Depression" was now in full force! Thompson Valley Reservoir was as dry as a feather bed. Groceries were scarce No Money! Many were desperate No Jobs! A lonely, hungry man walked to Lone Pine without shoes. He was walking with pieces of automobile tires under his feet. People from the drought stricken areas of this great nation were completely demoralized. Wayne Elder was working at Lone Pine for forty dollars a month and board. He purchased a new Chevrolet car; payments were thirty-five a month. Livestock were mortgaged. The Bank Of Lakeview allowed only a paltry few dollars each month to keep the ranch afloat. Sound good? Hell No! Two miles south of the Lone Pine Headquarters was a rutty, nasty stretch of road whenever it rained. One night, well after dark, while everyone was asleep, a knock was heard at the door. A U. S. Forest Service employee, Mr. Janick, walked that two miles in the rain. He was desperate. His car was in that mud hole. Slivers, holding a lighted candle, led him to a vacant bedroom. The next morning Slivers, with a team of horses, pulled his car from that unforgiving booby-trap-no charge. Everyone had breakfast. Mr. Janick went on his way. Needless to say they were good friends for many years, thereafter.

Frank Wyman, a distant cousin, had saved a few dollars. We talked at great lengths; and finally decided that both of us, working together, could do something different. After mature deliberation, we decided to purchase the Silver Lake Machine Shop. The shop also repaired automobiles. The business wasn't a thriving one during those depressing times. Example: Mel Freeman borrowed Floyd Lane's pickup truck to haul wood. The clutch failed! The truck was headed for the junkyard. We purchased parts and installed them for $20.00 in order that Freeman wouldn't be further embarrassed. He didn't have $20.00. We never received even a partial payment. James Harper had a broken down 1926 Nash car for sale. That vehicle, when repaired, would be good advertisement for our business. A year later the business had deteriorated further. We locked the doors. Wyman went back to his ranch.

Roy Hardisty and Maurice took a few blankets; and drove the Nash to Merrill, Oregon. We expected to find work there. The Nash had comfortable "fold down" seats for sleeping. Early one morning before the sun came up, a man called from the sidewalk with a loud voice. "Any of you guys want to go to work?" Our enthusiastic response was "Yeah!" They followed him in his new pickup to lower Klamath Lake bed. Mr. Liskey was a cattleman and grain farmer. After formal introductions, he said "This is my hay crew headquarters. Hardisty, you will be the cook for the hay crew." Emery, you will be the catskinner." He further stated that our three meals a day would cost us thirty-five cents per meal a day, each. Our wages were fifty cents an hour. Liskey had all the necessary equipment in place at the camp. Emery boarded a caterpillar. Another operator was aboard a tractor. A wire cable tied the two together about two hundred feet apart. The purpose was to dig a deep hole in the ground down to water, which would be a livestock watering hole. Midway between the caterpillar and tractor, a huge scoop was installed for moving the dirt from the bottom of the muddy hole. The caterpillar pulled the scoop full of mud to the top. The mud was automatically unloaded at the top of the hole. The tractor, going in the opposite direction, pulled the scoop backwards into the hole for the next load. One evening, the foreman on the job, drove to Klamath Falls for tractor parts. Hardisty, in one of his mischievous moods, had an idea. He brewed some tea and boiled some hotdogs. The tea was weak. He put the weak tea and hotdogs into a chamber pot and placed the pot under the foreman's bed. The foreman returned late the same evening and "Whoa!" he found the pot. The following day Liskey said: "I'm firing your partner. I suppose you will quit." The response was "Let him go!" The rainy season was headed our way, all rain, no work. No work, no income. Nine dollars and thirty-five cents in the hole each week. The job was short lived.

37

Wesley and Hazel Lee had a small delicatessen type store on South Sixth Street in Klamath Falls Around the early nineteen thirties, a dejected, weary looking young man walked into their store, with only one nickel. He was hungry. Hazel sold him one loaf of day old bread and three slices of balogna for that nickel. The Lee's were also vulnerable. Wes had a one and one-half ton Reo truck. Their store closed. They spent time at the Lone Pine ranch one winter. Wes bought whole-sale flour, sugar and other staples in truckload quantities. His deliveries were concentrated in the Silver Lake area.

Hollinshead brothers, Dean, Cecil and Chester, operated the stage and freight line between Bend and Lakeview. Dean Hollinshead and Chester Simmers, as partners, were known as Simmers and Hollinshead log hauling contractors. Maurice asked Dean if he had an opening for a new employee. Dean replied: "Yes, I do, go to Three Creeks and talk to Mr. Simmers right away. I'll tell him you are coming." Hallelujah! The garage and machine shop was, without mental reservation, or self evasion of mind in any way whatsoever, sold to Archie Deadmond. New and more profitable horizons loomed ahead. Previous to finalization of the sale, however, a meeting with Mr. Simmers was completely successful. He was a calm, dedicated and likeable man.

The logging camp at Three Creeks was primitive in many respects. Horses were used to "cross haul" the logs onto the truck-trailer combinations. Trucks were unloaded at Lenz railroad siding. At the siding, the logs were loaded onto railroad flat cars. The logs were shipped to Chiloquin Lumber Company in Chiloquin, Oregon. Maurice was now a truck driving log hauler. the pay was six dollars a day.

The six dollars a day included full maintenance of the truck assigned to your safekeeping. Board and room was on the house. Drivers called the truck, "my truck." Trucks were numbered. The numbers were necessary for the scaler's bookkeeping. The logging procedure was severely curtailed for approximately three months every-winter. Once again, the paycheck was non-existent. The money saved from the three months as a truck driver looked like one million

Maurice and Slivers were not seeing eye to eye at this time. The ranching and cattle business did not appear to be sufficient for three or four families; when three boys were grown and decided their own fate. Slivers and Mother appeared to be at odds over something. No one knew why! Mother was a caring person, very enlightening, courageous, thoughtful and comfortable to be around. She was not a demanding person; but a typical hardworking housewife and mother, sound in mind and memory.

Grandmother Emery was visiting her daughter, Ethel Cody, in San Diego that winter. The Cody's really never felt the depression years as we did. Bill Cody was an officer with the San Diego police department. The Cody's had one child, a daughter, Arlene. She was industrious, interested in genealogy and literature. She chose banking as her profession and was the manager of the First Interstate Bank of Springfield, Oregon. She compiled a genealogical history of the Emery and Cody families. When she retired, she moved to the Seattle, Washington, area to be near her son, Gregory and daughter, Michelle.

Grandfather Emery and son, George William Emery, were on the Buck Creek Ranch. I was with those two, intermittently while I was awaiting my next opportunity. Grandfather's other sons Russell, Jim, Ted, Frank and Wayne had gone their own way at that time. Elmer and Hema, Mother's parents, were visited many times that winter by this writer, grandson. They had five children, Esther, Frank, Ted, Austa and Neva, in that order. Granddad Grave's father, Cincinnatus, worked his way west from Connecticut to Idaho. His final resting place is in Pahsemori Valley, near Goldberg, Idaho.

38

Who was about to appear on the street in Bend, Oregon? Chet Simmers, that's who. He asked: "What are you doing this winter?" My response was "Nothing worth while." He said "Nothing huh? Come out to the ranch in Gilcrest and stay a couple of days." My response to him was "Good idea. I'll be there soon." When I arrived at Simmers' ranch, I perceived that he, like many others, was not overly secure financially. The Simmers had one son, Robert, and a very attractive daughter, Beulah. Mrs. Simmers, to me, was a second mother. Mrs. Simmer's son Robert, and daughter, Beulah moved to LaPine where they were going to school. Chet had a workshop, heated and well equipped for preparing the several logging trucks for the following season in the woods. He suggested, that we could prepare and overhaul them He said he didn't, however, have much money. That was O K with me. Herman Searman was the caretaker at the ranch. Herman's job was tending to the dairy herd and delivering the milk to town. Two months passed, the trucks were ready for hauling logs. The skies were clearing; and the future looked great.

1937 International logging truck.

The Chiloquin Lumber Company had established a complete new facility. It consisted of a cookhouse, a full time chef, housing for the employees, including Simmers and Hollinshead employees. The camp was near the foot of Mt. Mazama, Now it was time to go to work. The trees were cut, marked and loaded onto the trucks and hauled to the railroad. The railroad transported them to the sawmill in Chiloquin. The sawmill turned them into lumber. Employment, once again, was seasonal. Maurice had a 1937 Plymouth. He was not sure what the winter months ahead would contribute toward a paycheck. He and a co-worker named Whitey, decided to travel to Los Angeles and live in an apartment during the winter months. They had saved much of their summer wages. They planned to return to Chiloquin Camp the following spring; and work throughout the summer months. The first night in the Senator Hotel, Whitey quipped. "I know a lady here. Do you mind if I call her?" My response was "No, call her." Shortly thereafter, the young lady appeared at the hotel. Whitey asked "Do you object if the two of us go to a movie?" Once again, the response was: "No, go right ahead!" Two days later, Whitey appeared back at the hotel. He was filthy dirty and flat broke. He was offered ten dollars which he graciously accepted and we parted company.

39

Aircraft factories were beginning to hire new employees. Trouble was brewing in Europe. Germany posed a threat to all European Countries, possibly to the entire World. Moving to a metropolitan area was obviously frustrating. However, if steady work was the answer, and full time employment was available, why not go for it? Scrap metal had been shipped to Japan for years. Undoubtedly, we in this country, were unaware of their plans. Maurice applied for a job at Solar Aircraft Company and was accepted with one request. The company needed welders for manufacturing stainless steel exhaust manifolds. His previous experience was not comparable to the fine art of aircraft stainless steel and monel metals. Menial jobs in the factory were not his choice. The pay was twenty dollars per week. Fleet Welding School was attended vigorously for several months. One evening, after the night school classes, he approached his car. Who was sitting on the running board but Whitey. He had found my car. He was working for a crew of land surveyors. After our reunion that night, we had breakfast together many times. We finally lost contact with each other. His whereabouts today is unknown. Mrs. Cope ran a boarding house near the factory. Wow! The third boarding house in this young man's life. Maurice entered the production line at Solar. Hourly wages were increased substantially. A newly purchased red Buick car was envied by the boarding house occupants.

A beautiful young lady subsequently entered the young man's life. Her name was Yvonne. She was working in a corset shop at that time. We drove to her parents ranch in Julian, California to meet the family. There, Maurice met Yvonne's parents, Mr. and Mrs. Hellyer and son. Conversations and a slip of the tongue by Mrs. Hellyer throttled the conversation for a moment. Mrs. Hellyer said "Yvonne, do you remember the time you turned the dishpan full of dishes upside down and all the dishes went crashing to the floor?" The living room was extraordinarily quiet. You could have heard a pin drop ten miles down the road. Back in San Diego, Maurice went to the corset shop to see Yvonne. The owner was behind the counter. "Where is Yvonne?" The reply was: "Haven't you heard? She got married." Case closed, and out the door went a mortified young man.

40

A few months later, Mother called. She was in a hospital in Bend, Oregon. It was time to take a few days off and go to Bend and see Mother. She recovered nicely. Hal Blanchard, in Bend and unemployed, was completely disgusted, as were his wife and son, Larry. Hal was a first class mechanic. We talked about the possibilities existing in the aircraft industry. The two of us drove back to San Diego. Hal also applied for work at Solar. Five days later, he hadn't received a response from his application for employment. With his wry smile he said, "If I had a horse, I would ride back to Oregon." The sixth day the good news came. We would both be working together at Solar. His wife, Myrtle and son, Larry arrived a few days later. Hal Blanchard was eventually promoted to foreman. Larry, his son became a California Highway Patrolman. Aircraft parts were being produced at a rapid rate. A "For Sale" sign on a property at 2866 Madison Avenue in San Diego, looked attractive. Mr. Coulter owned that small two bedroom home. He was asking two thousand six hundred fifty dollars with a down payment of five hundred dollars. Monthly payments of twenty dollars were to be made. A contract was signed. Mr. Coulter remarked "It is good to find a young man who has saved five hundred dollars."

A little known fact was that something of monumental proportions was looming over the horizan, Japan, in their quest for power, was planning an attack on Pearl Harbor. Their bombs fell on Pearl Harbor December 7, 1941. The devastating, unsolicited, horrendous act created an outcry from all who worked at Solar, at that time. The sight of P-38 fighter planes on that day gave only minimal comfort. A few days after the attack, a notice was placed on the company bulletin board for two employees, knowledgeable in the company's procedure, to volunteer for the new assignment. Fourteen men volunteered. Chauncey Martin and Maurice Emery were selected. Additional manufacturing facilities were available at the Edward G. Budd Manufacturing Company in Philadelphia, Pennsylvania. The two selected were to be supervisors in that distant facility. Their choice to do so was none less than patriotic. Maurice chose to entrust Mrs. Cody, his aunt, with his home and car. He was riding the Santa Fe "Super Chief" train across the country to his future, new job. Boarding a shuttle train in San Diego transferring to the Sante Fe "Super Chief" in Los Angeles, we were well on the way. Near the California-Arizona border the train was delayed four hours. A terrific rainstorm had damaged the railroad tracks ahead. The train wasn't moving. Anxiety existed. The conductor assured the passengers that we would undoubtedly make up some of the loss before arriving in Chicago. We were only thirty minutes behind schedule. The coal fired engine, with its powerful, eight foot high drive wheels, reassured us that we would, indeed, make up time. We were unaware that the comfortable lounge, dining and sleeping cars in which we were riding, had been previously manufactured by the "soon to be" employer. Maurice arrived without a topcoat. He was wearing flimsy Southern California clothing; and carrying two suitcases. Seventeen inches of snow on the ground wasn't comparable to Southern California climate. That was December 23, 1941. A taxi whisked him to the nearest hotel, where he spent his first night in the City of Brotherly Love.

Chauncey Martin with his wife and son arrived by car. Their stay in Philadelphia was a short one. Mrs. Martin was dissatisfied with her surrounding environment. Chauncey was displeased with his assignments at work. After their three months stay, they returned to California. Maurice's job was training existing employees in the more intricate work of airplane parts for bombers, fighters, and training planes. A super challenge ahead! The company was a manufacturer of railway passenger cars. It was also one of the larger automobile components parts suppliers in America. One third of the nation's passenger cars were built at the Company as of 1953.

41

An acquaintance back in California, Ross Smith, had a brother who lived in Philadelphia. His name was Harry Smith. He had a daughter named Vivian. Vivian had recently graduated from Frankfort Hospital as a registered nurse.

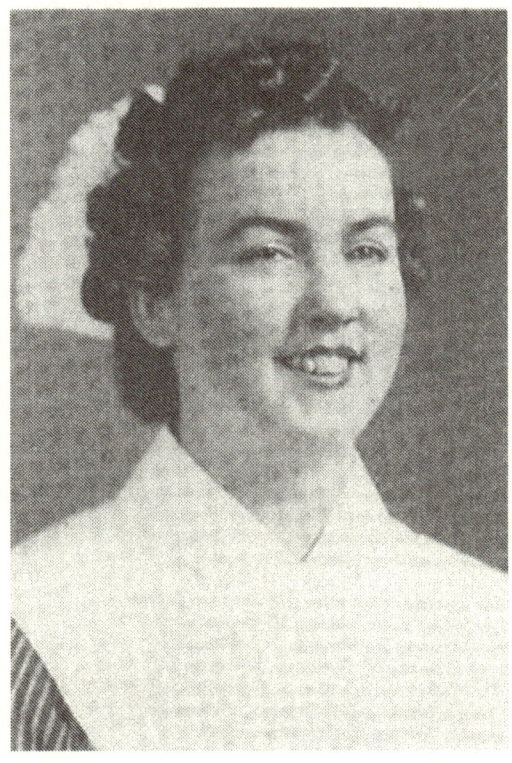

Vivian, graduate of Frankford Hospital School of Nursing

Her poise was outstanding. Vivian had personality plus, a nice family and many friends. Attraction for each other was mutual. Several months later, Maurice and Vivian were married on September 17, 1942. We lived in a Venango Street Apartment for several months. Gasoline was rationed. Coffee and sugar were also rationed. Vivian was a visiting nurse for two years during World War Two. She believed that it was the patriotic thing to do. Her work took her to various parts of the city. Visiting nurses' uniforms were medium blue in color with a head piece to match. She looked great. Public transportation was her only transportation. The honeymoon was a combination business and pleasure trip. The company needed a representative in Detroit, Michigan, to observe some tooling at a General Motors Plant on Grand Avenue. We boarded the train bound for New York City and spent the first night at the Waldorf Astoria in New York City. The company arranged for accommodations at the Hotel Leland in Detroit. Business was completed at the General Motors Plant and we were homeward bound. Maurice returned to his work with the Company. Training existing and new employees was a strenuous task. Vocational schools, Mastbaum and Dobbins came to our aid. Students received their basics at those schools. The larger and final instructions were taught at the Budd school. Many of these employees were honored with a supervisory status.

Each employee, having been certified by Air force and Navy inspectors, was permitted to perform his operations on a "piece work" basis. The more they produced, the larger their paycheck each Friday. The company did not pay an hourly wage at that time. The company was selected and received a contract to build all stainless steel cargo transport airplanes. The Federal Government built and provided all new facilities. One of the buildings was seventeen acres in size. These facilities, at a later date, were used to manufacture railway passenger cars also made of stainless steel.

The employees consisted of women, older men, and those who couldn't hear or talk—they sort of mumbled. Maurice became quite adept at sign language. Needless to say, these were exceptionally good workmen. Race, creed, and, or color were not a factor. A Mr. Rogers was a general foreman and often sounded off with derogatory remarks about the women, all of whom, wore blue baggy coveralls. He was a man of medium stature, consequently a group of the more powerful women "nailed" Mr. Rogers, as he was passing by the ladies rest room. His clothes were removed and he was "out the door" for everyone to see. The management was not especially happy for some time. General foremen, with "know how" were not easy to find. This incident caused Mr. Rogers to reevaluate his position; and to treat the women with more respect.

The better employees would earn up to $40.00 for an eight hour shift, providing their work was satisfactory. A man, by the name of Huey Brooks, was unable to keep up with the women; and had to be questioned about his unsatisfactory workmanship. This was also my job. A day or two after I had reprimanded him, he met me and retorted "Emery, I all most knocked you on your ass." My reply to him was "Yes, you might have floored me, however, on the other hand, I might have gotten off the floor and beaten the hell out of you; and you'd be like a frozen flea in an iceberg at the north pole." Following this exchange of pleasantries, our relationship was immensely improved.

42

Walter Buick and Frank Emery entered the armed services during the early nineteen forties. Buick and Emery were stationed in Fort Riley, Kansas. During the training, standing at attention, Frank broke the line. His behavior was urgent. He had to relieve himself. The Sergeant raked him over the coals in the usual fashion. The Sergeant's demand was brutal. Frank was ordered to stand at attention and repeat the words "I will not break ranks again "five hundred times. Soon thereafter, he was discharged. He returned to scenic Oregon. Walter was stationed at a base in Georgia, preparing to "ship out," to the European theatre. His homesickness was overpowering. He boarded a train, and on leave, he was headed to Philadelphia. The only person on the East Coast he had previously known was Maurice Emery. Three days later and heading back to Georgia, he repeated the words, "I'll kill every damn German I can find." Unfortunately, Walter was shot and seriously injured on the beaches during the Normandy invasion. Walter wrote, from his hospital bed asking for a fountain pen. The pen was hurriedly placed in the mail to the hospital where he was confined. A couple of weeks later the pen was returned with the word, "deceased." A plaque honoring this heroic young man stands beside the courthouse in Klamath Falls

J, S. Martin & Sons' grocery store was located across the street from the Linebaugh and Groth General Merchandise Store. Mrs. Martin's son, Nelson Smith, Was stationed at Fort Dix, New Jersey. Meeting this soldier in downtown Philadelphia was a pleasure. Nelson, more than six foot tall, skinny as a toothpick and happy as usual. His tan uniform and matching head-wear transformed him from a kid roaming the streets of Silver Lake to a real fighter. Nelson wasn't sent over seas as a fighting man. He was transferred back to the West Coast for other reasons. After the war he was a post master, for thirty years, at Petaluma, California until his death sometime around the late 1970's or early 1980's. The whereabouts of his family and distinguished wife are presently unknown. Mrs. Nelson was a former Nebraska schoolgirl.

Fred Alsdorf was also another enlisted army man during World War Two. Fred told of his many encounters while in the service of his country. These were explained after his return, at an annual meeting in Fort Rock, Oregon. The Fort Rock Homesteaders Association meets yearly. Many discussions followed during this harmonious gathering. At one of these discussions of the Homesteaders he spoke these words "While in France during the War under General George "Blood and guts" Patton, I was privileged to know him personally!" "The General went all out for his fighting soldiers. We underlings played cards with the General when opportunities arose. Patten loved his men."

Bill Burton, son of Henry and Bessie Bolliger Burton was lost but not forgotten. He, we understand, was in the United States Navy. Bill's sister Mary Burton Redfield lives in Lakeview, Oregon. She was the librarian for many years. Information regarding these two is marginal. To further elaborate, at this time, would be ineffective unless proven otherwise.

43

Each time I received notice from the draft board that my presence was required, the company would send the personnel manager, Claude Clymer, with me: and he would secure yet another deferment. My draft classification remained 1-A during the entire war. These deferments caused me to feel guilty; because I was not helping the war as much as desired. Two of my uncles, Wayne Emery and Ted Emery were carpenters during construction of housing for Japanese Americans. This housing was constructed near the Oregon-California border South of Klamath Falls, Oregon. Wayne was later in the Army in the Pacific. He was detained as a prisoner of war in the Pacific for several years. He returned home much like a "broken old man."

Several times friends and acquaintances suggested that I might have a 4F classification. These suggestions were humiliating and degrading. In response, and in each instance, I would allow them to view my draft card with the 1A classification. Previous to the war's ending, my desire to go abroad with a side arm and rifle, was overwhelming. Near the end of these great conflicts; all the "tail enders" were rounded up for a stint in some part of the services-who knows, Army, Navy, Air Force, etc. We were taken to the Armory in Philadelphia, to a huge hanger with huge doors at each end. Our instructions were: "Form a circle, take off your clothing and march around in a circle." At this time, the doors were opened. It was really brutally cold with a strong north wind. After some of this nude marching, we were all ready for combat, fox holes, or anything to get away from that freezing cold wind. No one from this group was drafted, as the war came to an abrupt end.

44

The War was over; and the next move was into a gray iron foundry as a mill-wright supervisor. We were now using some kinds of scrap metal which had formerly been shipped to Japan for their benefit in the 1930's. Now we were using some of these cast off metals, ourselves. We were making brake drums for Ford Motor Company. Sand, sea coal, molten metal, and other materials were cast about. Foundry work was a tough job. We had a new home and acreage in Southampton, Pennsylvania. We raised strawberries for the commercial markets on this acreage. Prior to the strawberry activity, we had purchased a dairy farm near Tunkhannock, Pennsylvania. This dairy farm was operated by a man named Henry Severcool. It was a good weekend retreat. It was secluded, had better air, clean water, hunting and fishing and was incredibly peaceful.

Mother and her sister, Austa Carlon, drove to Southampton in 1947. They stayed one month with us. We took them to a Lake George, New York Resort for a few days. During their stay, they were shown the many sights in New York City and many interesting places. Mother and Aunt Austa returned home, Mother to Lone Pine and Aunt Austa to her home in Burns, Oregon. Curiosity as to the whereabouts of Chester and Betty McCall was important. Chester was a next door neighbor (bookworm) back in Oregon, during the early nineteen twenties. He and his wife, Betty, had relocated in New York City. Their well documented past disclosed many events that had occurred after their departure from Silver Lake, Oregon. They had two sons and lived in a ten room apartment in the Big Apple while he was working for the editor of Time Magazine. Aunt Austa had communicated with Chester and Betty since their college days. She told Maurice that Chester and Betty had relocated to a suburb of Washington D. C. Maurice telephoned Chester to ascertain the name of the suburb where he and Betty lived. Chester told him that they lived in Chevy Chase, Maryland; and invited them to visit. Chester was at the station to meet us. Chester was a very distinguished looking gentleman. He was wearing a derby hat, spats and carrying a cane; significantly different than his boyhood attire. The cane dangling from his left arm, was for "show purposes" only. Their Hamilton Style home in Chevy Chase, was in an exclusive area, nicely landscaped with beautiful surroundings, in "apple pie" order. During our visit with Chester and Betty, we were shown newspaper clippings and pictures of Chester and Betty on the Presidential Yacht with Franklin and Eleanor Roosevelt The newspaper article stated that Roosevelt said "Chester, I believe you will become president one day." He was a member of the school board in Chevy Chase. He had been a purchasing agent for the U. S. Army during World War Two. Before leaving for home, Chester took us to his Washington D. C. office on one of the top floors of a "high rise" building. The name, Chester H. McCall, was emblazoned on the entrance door. That man was not a "phoney!"

45

We visited the family back at the Lone Pine Ranch, after a ten year absence. The cattle business was much improved The partnership had sold seventy-five thousand dollars worth of feeder cattle in nineteen thirty nine. One twelve hundred pound steer sold for five cents a pound. That amounted to sixty dollars on the hoof. The smaller ones, obviously sold for more than that amount per pound. That was real money at that time. A nineteen thirty nine Buick Century was purchased. A red one, looked like a "gangster" car at that time. Horse drawn equipment was now obsolete. Two new gasoline powered tractors were purchased; one was a Fordson and the other an Allis Chalmers.

Back in Pennsylvania the name, Edward G. Budd Manufacturing Company, had been changed to, The Budd Company.

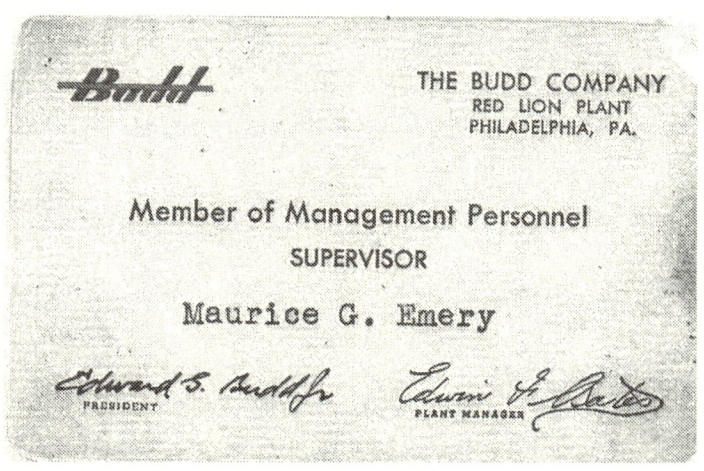

Maurice was sixteen years with the Budd Company

A new assignment was in order. Maurice needed more knowledge for his work. The long, tiring nights at Temple University Metallurgy Classes were taught five nights a week. There, he was taught the chemical compositions of steel and the art of separating metals from their ores, heat treatment et cetera. His new title was Materials and Process Engineer. The prime factors in producing a satisfactory product that will give maximum, trouble free performance, of materials and processing methods used in its manufacture. Quality can not be tacked onto it: Integrity must be built into the product. It is the function of the Materials and Process Engineer to bridge this gap to minimize design errors and production delays. Engineering design is responsible to the government contracting agency for meeting its design specifications.

Technical groups, to accomplish this are composed of chemists, metallurgists, physicists, engineers and technicians. Only specialists such as the process engineers can determine and furnish the knowledge to the proper fields. The materials group, for instance, tests incoming materials to determine if they meet government and manufacturers requirements. The metallurgical group is concerned with every piece of incoming metal used in a finished product. Physical properties may be improved with heat treatment, the machining and forming of the metal, and the radii of its bends. Tinius-Olson machines test physical qualities of material by indicating point of failure.

Vickers metallographic microscopes evaluate metallic structures. X-ray machines expose the interior of welds for unsafe defects. Chemical, plastics and fasteners are thoroughly examined prior to their usage. Engineers are the "Doctors of Industry." Maurice was now working at the newly built location, continuing as a supervisor. The main seventeen acre Budd Company building was separate from the office and maintenance buildings. The new Budd Company building was used for railway car, truck cargo bodies and airplane engine parts manufacturing. Jet engines for airplanes were fast becoming a reality. The Budd Company manufactured coaches, dining cars and sleeping cars for most of America's railway needs. Subway cars were built and sold to New York City and London, England. Approximately one third of the Nation's new railway cars were built at Budd, as of 1953. The truck bodies were sold world wide. Jet engine parts were made for Curtis Wright, Pratt & Whitney and General Electric Companies. Those companies assembled Budd made parts for installation on new jetliner planes.

46

Mail and telephone conversations from Oregon were looked forward to with great anticipation. The Lone Pine Ranch was expanding. Slivers had purchased the Owsley Ranch on Bridge Creek.

Stacking hay with the handyman hay stacker at the Owsley Ranch

Clifford Dale Emery—1946

Branding calves at the Owsley Ranch

Dale Emery and Lucile Egli were married November 14, 1942. The newly purchased ranch was their part of the business. They had two daughters, Zelda Gay and Cherri Lynn. The Owsley Ranch had remarkable effects on the Lone

Pine operation. The Owsley branding iron was purchased with the sale. It was called Royal Crown iron. The Sled Runner iron was abandoned. The new company was called the Royal Crown Cattle Company. No longer indebted to the Bank Of Lakeview, prosperity was "Just around the corner." Though the years, Slivers and Esther had become more estranged. They divorced; and Slivers made his headquarters in Klamath Falls and Klamath Marsh. Esther remained at the Lone Pine Ranch. Slivers, Dale, and Kenneth were partners in the Royal Crown Cattle Company. Lightening had struck the lone pine tree many times. The dead tree finally hit the ground. Lone Pine had lost much of It's identity.

Early one morning at the Owsley Ranch, in nineteen forty-nine, the weather was colder than usual. Fire wood was placed inside the heating stove and lighted for the exceptionally cold day. Between the living room ceiling and the roof above, a spark ignited the wooden structure. Insulation was on fire and the house was about to burn. Dale climbed to the roof with a garden hose in an attempt to extinguish the flames coming through the roof. Most homes had fire extinguishers suspended from the ceilings, around each and every heating or cook stove. The extinguishers contained carbon tetrachloride. The combination of water, chloride, smoke and fire, when inhaled, is exceptionally dangerous. Dale's lungs were affected. His health was being jeopardized. He extinguished the fire, at a cost, which left him impaired for his remaining years. The weather was very cold in the winter of nineteen fifty-one; and Dale was having trouble breathing. He decided he would go to Safford, Arizona to ascertain if the warmer weather would be beneficial. The following winter he and Lucile and their daughters, Zelda and Cherri returned to Safford and Phoenix, Arizona. The warmer climate didn't improve his deteriorating health. The family returned to the Owsley Ranch and discussed their next move. In nineteen fifty-three, they decided to relocate in Corning, California

47

Vivian had previously had two ectopic pregnancies. Therefore, she was unable forever after, to bear a child. Maurice and Vivian decided to adopt either a boy or girl. Vivian was working for a doctor. One of the doctor's patients was giving her soon to be born child up for adoption. That was an emotional and saddening experience. We joined the mother on the hospital steps; and she handed over the nine day old baby to us. She was born December 25, 1949. We named her Beryll Lea. We discovered, early in her childhood, that she had an emotional problem. She had problems in school and with other children. We took her to several different doctors; but they were unable to help.

Walter Brown, a former Budd Company employee, was presently working for Douglas Aircraft Company in California. Walter called and said the company had an opening in the Materials and Process Engineering Department. He further inquired "Would you be interested?" My reply was "I'll think about that" He called the next day and said his boss, Mr. Adrian Bibbee, was in Atlantic City, New Jersey. Mr. Bibbee was hiring, if possible, knowledgeable employees from the East Coast to work in California. Maurice drove to Atlantic City, resume in hand, for an interview. He was hired the same day. A contract was also signed. Once again, monumental decisions were in order. Vivian was in agreement. She theorized that the move to California would be an appropriate one. Work at the Budd Company was terminated.

The dairy farm was sold to Mr. Ray Willis, a single man. Mr. Willis's mother was also involved in the purchase. We had sold our home in Southampton; and were, once again, living in Philadelphia, on Vista street. This new assignment at Douglas was to establish criteria for materials and processes, analysis of failures and defective parts and control of processing operations of naval aircraft. The job title was materials and process analysis of failures and defective parts and control of processing operations of naval aircraft. The job title was Materials and Process Engineer. We were working with current problems concerning aluminum, magnesium, titanium and high temperature alloys. Low alloy steels, stainless steels and ultra high strength steels were used.

Maurice was subsequently transferred to another facility in Torrance. That division was assigned a contract to build anti-missile motor cases. Employees working on the project had a secret and top secret status. Maurice had previously joined the Hollywood film Players Club for a little diversification from strenuous work. Evenings at the club and weekends on location at Palmdale, California were comforting. He soon learned that only five percent of those paying dues to the Screen Actors Guild were successful in the entertainment world. That too, was hard work

Sheriff Emery on location Hollywood film players, Palmdale, California

A cartoonist's observation of a would be actor.

Five years had passed at Douglas. the horizon looking north appeared to be cleaner than the contaminates around the Los Angeles area. Retirement at age forty-five wasn't the answer. Possibilities in Corning, California looked great, if one was willing to work. Working in the industrial world for more than twenty years, made it seem like another change was due. Monday morning a written resignation was handed to the supervisors. With reluctance, the resignation was accepted. A dinner the following day left no doubt as to the next move.

48

A weekend trip to Corning was in order. Vivian was in Florida with her terminally ill mother. Wes and Jean Havens were taking care of daughter, Beryl, during the daytime. With the Havens, we drove to Corning; and found that Dale, Lucile and daughters, Zelda and Cherri, had purchased a combination motel and gift shop. The combination of the fire and ill health convinced them to move to that warmer climate. Dale had suggested that we buy a ten acre parcel within the City limits. It was there we were to spend the next twenty-seven years. We purchased the ten acres. The ten acre parcel had a run down home and a large barn. The house needed extensive renovation. The improvements were made in haste; and made livable in a very short time. There were several vacant building lots in the City. We purchased three of those for a total cost of eleven hundred dollars. Three new homes were constructed on these lots. We built the homes in their entirety, including plumbing and electric wiring. Those homes were sold soon after construction was completed.

The next project and purchase was in Corning. A two story building was for sale. The building was originally the Tehama County Savings Bank, later Bank of Italy. It lost its identity when it became Bank of America. The bank was renovated for a florist shop. The florist shop is, forty-two years later, still doing business at that location. The vault serves as a refrigerated cooling room for flowers. Following the bank building rejuvenation, a former vacated restaurant building was purchased, renovated and served as a Sears outlet store. An abandoned bakery building was bought, and reconstructed. A Pizza parlor was constructed in the larger area of the building. A beauty parlor was constructed in one corner of the same building. The building was completely renovated with new electric, plumbing, light fixtures, paint and floors. The building was later sold to Bank of America. Demolition followed. A new bank is now well established in that location.

The third and most controversial purchase was an abandoned blacksmith shop. Many of the elderly women in town cried to the high Heavens. They wanted it to be preserved as an historical museum. No Way! That falling down "junk pile" was hauled away to the city dump. The former blacksmith site, with a new building, was now the new home of the Corning District Chamber of Commerce. Maurice Emery was the Secretary Manager of the Chamber of Commerce.

Jones Insurance occupied part of the new building. Robert Jones Insurance still continues as a thriving business as of the year 2001. A vacant building was purchased in the downtown section. renovation was completed. A happy couple, Richard and Joyce Stark, established a successful refrigeration and cooling business in that building. The owner of a building, occupied by Inns Printing, wanted to sell. The purchase was a welcome one. Minor overhaul pleased Mr. Inns no end. A new building consisting of nearly six thousand square feet for a furniture and appliance center was built by Davies Construction for Emery. The building is presently occupied by Les Schwab Tire and Service Center. The seven above mentioned commercial properties were a pleasure to see. Moreover, they were an improvement for the City of Corning.

49

Prior to the time the Emery family left the East Coast and moved to Torrance, California, Esther left the Lone Pine Ranch and established her home in Redmond, Oregon. Soon after her departure, Kenneth Married Dorothy Morrison of Eugene, Oregon. They were married in Las Vegas, Nevada, October 18, 1955. They lived at the Lone Pine Ranch until the original Duncan house burned to the ground in 1961. They lived in Silver Lake until a new home could be built on the Lone Pine ranch. A new house was constructed in 1964. Back at Lone Pine in their new home, everything was going great until the new house burned to the ground. A new home in Silver Lake was their home for the remaining years of their lives. Kenneth and Dorothy had a daughter, Tina Gay and a son, Bruce. Tina was born while they were still living in the Duncan house and Bruce was born in 1962 before the new house was built in 1964.

Dale and Lucile were living in Corning and operating the motel and gift shop. Dale's health was not improving. Esther came to Corning to visit Maurice and Dale and their families. While she was there, the decision was made to find the best possible doctor for Dale. Dr. Smart of Los Angeles, California, was chosen. He was Winston Churchill's doctor for a similar condition. Churchill's condition was not nearly as severe, however. Dr. Smart said, "We cannot give you a new lung yet." His words were over emphasized on the word "yet." Dale was hospitalized for a few days and released to go home with a prescription for oxygen. He remained on Oxygen for the remainder of his life.

50

Maurice was on location in Palmdale, California, when he received a phone call from Vivian. Slivers had a horrible accident at Klamath Marsh. He was hauling a bull in a truck. The bull began climbing out over the truck cab. With the door open, Slivers stood on the running board, with hat in hand, attempting to quiet the animal. The truck was moving. He slipped and fell under the truck and was ran over. He died May, 31, 1960 in a Klamath Falls hospital. He was buried in the Silver Lake Cemetery on June 2, 1960 on Maurice's forty-fourth birthday. Now was a good time to return to Lone Pine and Klamath Marsh.

Maurice Emery back in the saddle again.

The purpose of the return was to help Brother Kenneth reorganize what was now the Royal Crown Cattle Company. We cleared fence right of ways; so fences could be reconstructed at the ranch. Discarded railroad ties were hauled from Lenz Station. We bought the ties for fifty cents each. We hired a man and a bulldozer to clear the right of way for new fences. When the work was completed, Maurice returned to Corning and found that Dale was slipping. His condition continued to worsen and he passed away September 10, 1962. He was laid to rest in the Sunset Hill Cemetery in Corning.

The Marsh summer cabin was never finished in 1933. Ernie Samson and Bert Wyman had built the log house during the great depression for the Emery's on Klamath Marsh. The logs were felled, debarked and hauled to the existing site in 1933. Horse drawn wagons were used to transport the logs. Samson and Wyman, experienced woodsmen, notched and rolled the logs one on top of the other. A porch on the east side covered the width of the house. Another porch covered about one half of the south side. Both were under the same roof. The roof was a pole raftered one. Poles were covered with used lumber from a demolished school house in Summer Lake. A shake roof covered the used lumber. Money was tight. The cabin was virtually unused for thirty years. Maurice spent the entire summer modernizing the structure. A huge five foot fireplace was erected on the south side. New flooring through out the structure was necessary. The kitchen, bathroom and windows were modernized. The renovation was completed in four months

Kenneth and Dorothy the second generation at Lone Pine

A New home at Lone Pine was the next project in 1964. It was a three bed-room, two bath with full size basement. Maurice, with the help of one ranch hand, built the home, with one exception. Jack Jones built two fireplaces, one in the living room and one in the basement. Jack was a professional in design work. A staircase type of spiraling structure for both fireplaces left only one chimney on top of the roof. The summer, nineteen sixty-four, was well spent, once again, at Lone Pine.

51

Maurice and Vivian had long desired a new home. They bought a five acre parcel directly across the street from the ten acre parcel where they had lived since moving to Corning. It was purchased from the Kirkpatrics, who moved to Fort Bragg, California, shortly thereafter. A new home on this five acre parcel was our goal. Construction of a hundred foot long ranch style home began in 1965. It was completed in 1966. Previous to its completion, a letter was received from a former co-worker at the Budd Company in Philadelphia. His name was Sam Horst. Mr. Horst and three other co-workers had accepted employment in Calcutta, India. Their work was to be with the Hindustan Motor Company. A three year contract was necessary. The four co-workers suggested Emery as the fifth to go to that foreign land. The position was not considered to be worthwhile. Foreigners working in that far away land would be at a tremendous disadvantage. Requirements were strict. A three year contract would be required. A three years' supply of toilet paper from your country would be required. You, at that time, would live in a compound. You would be chauffeured to and from a local grocery store. The reply to Mr. Horst was "Thanks! but no thanks!"

The new home was completed Income from the rental properties was adequate. Chamber of Commerce activities were not overly time consuming. January 26, 1978, election results revealed that Emery was now a Corning City Councilman and Secretary Manager of the Corning District Chamber of Commerce. Activities were not overly time consuming. January 26, 1978, election results revealed that Emery was now a Corning City Councilman and Secretary Manager of the Corning District Chamber of Commerce. Many "bumps on the head" followed.

Recitation of Abraham Lincoln's Gettysburg Address to new immigrants

Emery was airport commissioner, police commissioner and overseer of animal control.

The cartoon was published in the Corning Daily Observer Newspaper
July 30, 1969

Disgruntled citizens apply pressure from all angles. Those who love their work are never distracted from their duties. In 1972, Maurice was a candidate for Tehama County Supervisor against incumbent, Shan Patterson. Patterson was ending his first term in Tehama county, as Supervisor. Many voters suggested that Patterson deserved a second term. Patterson won with fifty-two percent versus Emery's forty-eight percent of the votes case. Emery was the loser. Emery was the political writer for the Corning Daily Observer newspaper. The secret to being a newspaper reporter is: "Lots of patience." Unhappy people grit their teeth and follow with a slurring remark: You say "Yes sir" or "Yes Ma'am." That is the way you indicate you are only doing your job.

Adjacent to a railroad siding in Richfield, there was a vacated property formerly administered by the U. S. Government, during the Korean War. Several buildings were empty. One building consisted of eighty thousand square feet. None of the buildings were on Tehama County tax rolls. Harold T "Bizz" Johnson was the congressman from our district. Correspondence from Mr. Johnson assured the Chamber of Commerce in Corning that the property could not be sold. His remarks struck a vital chord. The property was in the hands of the General Services Administration in Washington D. C. The Board of Directors approved a motion to send the Chamber of Commerce Manager to Washington D. C. for further inquiry. A tip suggested our representative contact Ralph Nader. Nader referred the Chamber Secretary to Fairfax O'Leary. O'Leary arranged a meeting with Arthur Samson, General Services Administrator. We were seated around a huge oak table for the meeting. At the close of the meeting, Mr. Samson said, "Mr. Emery, we will sell the property to the highest bidder." An exuberant Chamber Manager returned to Corning. He was well received at home. The property was sold: and hopefully the property, at this writing, is on the tax rolls. While in Washington D. C., the fifty-seventh annual meeting of the United States Chamber of Commerce was held. The small town maverick hosted Congressman Johnson and Senator Murphy at the annual dinner meeting. A good time was had by all.

52

February 14, 1972, Emery submitted his resignation to the directors of the Chamber of Commerce. He was a retired "free lancer." Rod Senter was a Corning City Councilman in Nineteen Seventy-two. His company transferred him to Clear Lake, California. His departure created a vacancy. Councilmen, at that time, considered asking former Councilman Emery to fill the vacant seat. Their suggestion was honorably received and dutifully acknowledged. Total time as City Councilman was seven years.

A high roller Ford dealership in Chico, California placed an add in the paper for salesmen. Good idea, Maybe! Needless to say, the company was after new business; or any business. If you were seen talking to a rag picker on the street, the company asked that you bring him to the main office. Several similar incidents occurred. The pay was less than normal. Their high pressure was more than normal. It appeared that the company was hiring many salesmen hoping that they would sell cars to their friends and family. Good by Ford dealership! That job lasted for a mere thirty days.

Lyndon Johnson Motors in Corning, established a dealership in Paradise, California. Mr. Johnson called and asked "Would you be willing to go to Paradise and work at the dealership?" My reply was "Yes, I would." The daily one hundred mile round trip to Paradise was a pleasant and scenic drive. I enjoyed my experience and work as an automobile salesman. Mr. Johnson had leased the former Ray Gillley lot and sales room. One early morning, Mr. Gilley drove his car to the rear of the dealership, gun in hand, and shot himself in the head. After the funeral, Johnson closed the dealership.

Back in Corning, the doctors recommended that Vivian have a hysterectomy. Arrangements were made at Community Hospital in Chico, California. The operation went well, however, she was given a blood transfusion before leaving the operating room. The following day she was in intensive care. The Doctor had given her reverse dialysis. She remained in intensive care the next five days. She never regained consciousness and died on September 26, 1980. The surgeon stated "Her body would not accept the blood transfusion given on the day of the operation." He further stated, "We tried our very best. We gave her reverse dialysis several times." She was normal and healthy at sixty-three and free from pain.

Many in Corning believed that she had been given the wrong type of blood. Maurice also thought she had been given the wrong type of blood. I was devastated. I felt alone and robbed of my mate. I also believed that $12,000.00 was an enormous price to pay for the wrong blood.

I retired; and sold the home and all commercial properties in Corning. Mother was terminally ill with cancer in Redmond, Oregon. I believed it was my obligation to care for mother. I went to Redmond and cared for her in her home for two and one-half years until her death on September 18, 1986. She was nearly 91 years of age. Daughter, Beryl passed away at age thirty four. She had cancer and died in a hospital in Bend, Oregon in 1984.

53

At this juncture in life, it appeared to be a lonely world. A new pickup truck and a new travel trailer were purchased. Friends and acquaintances spent their winters in Mesa, Arizona. That sounded like a good idea. The winters in Arizona are much better than the cool climates farther north. Square dancing in Arizona and Bend, Oregon, was finally achieved whenever a partner was found. I had a desire to travel; so I packed my thirty-five foot travel trailer and headed for Alaska. I crossed by ferry from Port Angeles, Washington to Victoria, Canada. I toured the beautiful Butchart Gardens for one day. I drove the entire length of Vancouver Island to Port Hardy. I took the Ferry from Port Hardy to Prince Rupert. The ferry was loaded. The Yellowstone Highway to Haines, Alaska, was most scenic. The long drive from Haines to Fairbanks was also a scenic drive. The outdoor salmon cook outs were delicious in their entirety. From Fairbanks, through Denali Park, to Anchorage was also a wonderful drive. The thirty-five foot travel trailer comfortably followed the three quarter ton pickup truck. Homer, Alaska, was a sight to behold. Fishermen standing shoulder to shoulder on the bank of the river, were fishing; and competing with the bear who were also fishing, was a sight for everyone to see. The Alaska pipeline ends at Valdez. The crude is loaded onto ships and transported to refineries elsewhere. The Alaska pipeline is custom designed for wild life to pass comfortably under the fast flowing crude oil. Your ear, when pressed to the pipeline, hears the gushing oil swiftly passing by. Alaska is huge. Everyone should see that mighty state. A wonderful trip for more than five thousand miles was enjoyed immensely before returning to Redmond, Oregon.

54

Walter Blackburn, a single man, and myself were discussing a planned trip to the rock bound coast of Maine. We both had travel trailers. My remark to Walter: "Walt, why not go to Maine and eat lobsters?" He replied "When do we start?" Two travel trailers, with a single man in each trailer departed Oregon and headed to the coast of Maine. The third day out, we spent a few days in West Yellowstone Park. A square dance festival was in session there. The two single men were looking for dance partners. Walter went to one side of the hall. That prompted me to go to the other side. Soon he approached my side and exclaimed "I can't find a dance partner!" My reply was "you're on the wrong side of the hall" The two found partners and a good time was had in West Yellowstone Park. Traveling across the North Central Plains, we eventually stopped over night in Niagara Falls. That is where honeymooners spend much of their time "honeymooning!" We were walking along the sidewalk. Honeymooners, walking hand in hand, were everywhere. My question to Walt "Do you think the honeymooners think we are a newly married couple?" He answered with a distasteful look and exclaimed "No, they think you are my father!"

Across Vermont and New Hampshire, the scenery was exotic. Roadsides in Maine were littered with hot steaming crab pots. Fresh crab was freshly cooked and it was superb. Walt was stationed in Key West, Florida during World War Two. Key West was our next destination. Several overnight stops and Key West was in sight. Leaving Key West, our ultimate destination was Mesa, Arizona. We stopped in Houston, Texas, and found another dance festival. Arriving at the festival together and upon entering the hall, Walt disappeared. He was no where in sight. He was finally discovered behind a table with a lady selling tickets. The evening ended and the young lady said, "Morey, you'll have to go to Arizona by yourself, Walt is staying here!" "That Charmer!" We were scheduled to leave the next morning. We were parked near the Astrodome. House cats fought most of the night. The next morning it was suggested that we depart the "Cat Haven" and go to Arizona. Don't believe either of us has returned to Houston since that day.

55

Silver Ridge Resort in Mesa, Arizona was our home during the winter of 1988. We parted company the following spring; and each of us went in separate directions. Several months later we met and mused at great lengths. Yellowstone park, Niagara Falls, crab pots on the rock bound coast of Maine, Key West, Florida, and Houston, Texas, were thoroughly reiterated. Summer months in Oregon and winter months in Mesa, Arizona, were the only places to be. Many call us "snowbirds." Nothing wrong with living the life of a bird if it suits your pocketbook and your desires. Square dances and ballroom dances were among many of the activities. All of these activities, however, were not the typical life of a bird. The weekly senior dances were held at the Senior Center in Mesa. A thought occurred. Why not attend one? A second dance at the Center an unusual discovery was made. That was in 1992. There were two ladies who attracted attention. One had dark hair, the other had white hair. The white haired lady wouldn't divulge her name. However, patience invariably wins. The third night at the hall a more aggressive move was made. Her name was Mary Lou. Ah Ha! as before, Patience is the key to real success. Afton suggested the three of us attend a dance at another hall during the week. Good Idea! Afton said "We will have a seat for you at our table." Upon arrival at the hall, I perceived the seat next to Mary Lou was occupied by a gentleman unknown to me. Disillusioned, an unoccupied table was found. Wow! This was a disaster. Almost ready to leave and homeward bound When! who should appear at the table of a single seventy-five year old man? Mary Lou and Afton that's who! The gentleman seated in my originally designated chair was an uninvited one. We had a good laugh and from then on everything took a turn for the better.

This writer had to make a choice. Would his thoughts lead him in a direction toward Afton Green or Mary Lou Grade? The choice was Mary Lou. Courtship followed. Mary Lou was born in Canada; but her parents brought her back to Kansas when she was four years old. She was raised in Kansas and entered nurse's training after completing high school. She married Harold Cheever Holman, a farmer near Oxford, Kansas on October 11, 1940. They farmed and operated a custom wheat combining operation. They combined wheat from Texas to Canada for many years. He passed away December 12, 1969. They raised three children, Lona Marie, Harold Allan and Lenna Louise. Lenna Louise died of cancer in 1990 at the age of 39. A widow at 48, Mary Lou continued to manage the farm. Harold Allan and Lenna Louise finished college and Mary Lou was alone. She married Norris E. Grade in 1972 and they continued to live on the farm. Norris died in 1988; and Mary Lou came to Arizona in 1989. She is a good home maker, plays the piano, is an all round good citizen and a wonderful person. She taught me to play tennis when I was seventy-five years old and had never played tennis before. She said I was good for a 75 year old. We continued dating and marriage vows were taken in Apache Junction, Arizona.

The Emery's on vacation in Seattle, Washington.

The vows were witnessed by Afton Green and Emery Clave, January 14, 1993. Since January 1993, the Emery's have toured the East Coast, Florida, Texas and spent time in Kansas where Mary Lou still has farm business. Their summers have been spent in Coquille and Silver Lake, Oregon. One visit Kenneth and I were recalling stories of the past and Kenneth told about the time he and his good friend Pat McCauliff were cruising near Beaver Marsh. They spotted a deer along the side of the highway, no hunting license, not in season, they shot and killed the animal. They obviously had a couple of beers under their belts. Kenneth jumped from the car, cut the animal's throat and stood by. Pat drove on. The weather was cold and Kenneth didn't have a coat. Pat wasn't to be seen near their prized kill. Each time Pat drove by in a hurry, it was a "Swoooish" movement! He finally located both Kenneth and the prize kill. They loaded the animal and Kenneth enjoyed the comfort of the warm vehicle. We had been visiting in Silver Lake, Oregon, the summer of 1999 and had returned to our summer home in Coquille. A few days after our return, we received a call from Bruce. Kenneth had died. He, as many others have done, had choked to death on a piece of beef. He was aged seventy-five.

56

The Royal Crown Cattle business, throughout its entirety, has never looked to Forest Service or Bureau of Land Management for livestock grazing. Kenneth's son, Bruce, was now in charge of the Royal Crown Cattle Company.

Bruce and Penny Emery third generation at Lone Pine

Previous to his becoming head of the business, he married Penny Sexton from Klamath Falls. They have two sons, Kyle, born July 21, 1992 and Trent, born June 14, 1995. Bruce and Penny are the third generation of Emery's to inhabit the Lone Pine and Klamath Marsh properties. Their new home at Lone Pine was completed for occupancy, August 2, 1999. The bunk house was their home for several years. It is now abandoned.

Kyle Emery, age 9 years third generation at Lone Pine

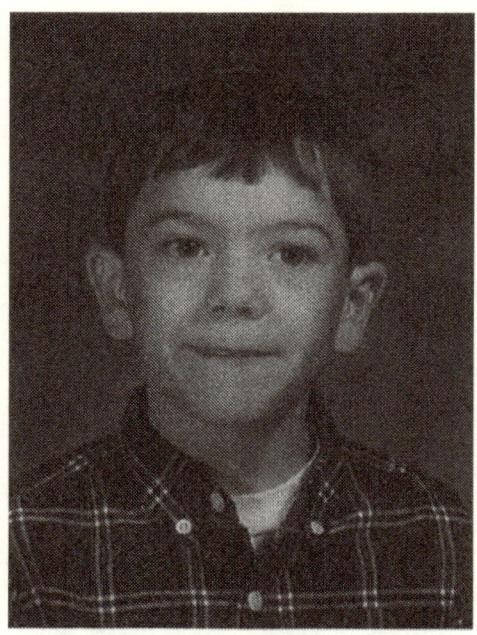

Trent Emery age 6 years fourth generation at Lone Pine

Bruce, in one of his more playful moods, captured two young coyotes and painted them with iridescent paint; took them to Klamath falls, at night, and turned them loose. The sight of the coyotes, at night, alarmed the dogs in town. All dogs were in an uproar. Klamath Falls residents were likewise alarmed. The total penalties, after proper identification of the perpetrator, have not yet been completely divulged. Another incident, concerning the prankster was near Lakeview. Bruce and a companion were driving along a gravel road. They passed a couple of hitch hikers. Within gravel throwing distance, they spun the car wheels. Gravel was thrown at the hikers. The hikers somehow identified the gravel throwers. The aftermath of this ordeal has never been properly revealed and acknowledged.

57

Insufficient moisture and short growing seasons (due to the higher altitude) caused a severe decline in farming and other activities. The general populace, during the early times, began their long evenings and nights with a hand held wax candle. Going from their places of abode to the outhouse was done mostly in darkness. The candle didn't serve well, especially when the wind was blowing. The kerosene lantern and the kerosene table lamp soon replaced the candle. The next improvement in lighting was the gasoline lantern and the gasoline table lamp. Gasoline, as used in the motorized vehicles, wasn't comparable to the more refined, smaller quantities necessary for satisfactory lantern and lamp performance. Following the battery powered flashlight, the next improvement was the air cooled, thirty-two volt Delco gasoline powered single cylinder generator and the Koehler water cooled four cylinder generator. Each generator charged a series of acid, water and lead batteries When the batteries were combined, thirty-two volt power was the result.

The Silver Lake Hotel had a more powerful four cylinder Koehler generator. That generator, when running, served more rooms with a single light suspended from the ceiling of each room. All lights were equipped with a pull chain. When it was nearly ten o'clock at night; and the gasoline engine was timed for a shut down "You better hurry and wash your face." A wash basin and a pitcher of cold water was awaiting you. The engine would stop; but the batteries would suffice until you crawled between the sheets and under the covers. Prior to the shut down, a few of the poker players from the Pastime Pool Hall could be seen scurrying to the nearby Silver Lake Hotel before the ten o'clock deadline. The more seasoned hardliners would continue until daylight.

Rural Electrification Administration was established May 11, 1935 to counteract some of the horrors of the Great Depression. It is unclear, at present, when ground was broken at LaPine, Oregon to head quarter the much needed power for the surrounding area. Phillip Pitman, a former Oregon State Highway Patrolman, had an idea. Pitman was a man of considerable wit and wisdom, an extraordinarily good spokesman and an extrovert to say the least. His idea was to bring electric power to the region. He went to Washington D. C.; and almost single handedly, convinced the R E A (Rural Electrification Administration) to bring electricity to the Silver Lake, Fort Rock and Christmas Lake regions.

58

Once again, the high desert country was about to flourish. Deep water wells were drilled. Sagebrush was beaten down. The ground was leveled and plowed, electric pumps were installed in the newly drilled wells and seeds were planted. Pivot and line sprinkling systems irrigated the new plantings. Alfalfa began to grow and flourish. New pole hay sheds were constructed to store the hay until it was sold. High protein alfalfa was baled and stored in these sheds along with oats, rye and barley awaiting the proper time for sale or for local use. Many of these products were transported, and still are, by semi-truck trailers, to other regions. Shipments overseas are not uncommon. The name, Christmas Lake was changed to Christmas Valley. New businesses were established. The lives of those living in the area were dramatically changed from the hard times of the early nineteen twenties and early thirties. Modern Day electricity has contributed greatly to Silver Lake and surrounding areas.

59

J. R. Simplot, the "Potato King," from Idaho, further developed much of the country-side around Silver Lake, Paisley and various other areas. He owns the Chewaucan Land & Cattle company, more commonly known as the Z X Ranch. A great entrepreneur and business man, is he. He is well known far and wide for his expertise. His interests include grain farming, feed lots, slaughter houses, potatoes and many more extensive operations. With a sense of pride, he further knows how to best manage his vast empire. His successes are many and varied. His neighbors are amazed at his many accomplishments.

The James L. Cliff ranch at Silver Lake is operated by J. L. Cliff's grand daughter, Teresa Cliff and her Mother, Ruth Cliff. However, the original ranch, from its inception, has grown tremendously. Many smaller ranches have been acquired over the years, by the Cliffs'. The J. D. (Jewel) Corum Ranch has also grown immensely from its meager beginnings. J. D's daughter, Marjorie (Marj) and husband, Bussy Iverson, along with their sons still continue to own and manage the business. There are, at present, only nine of the original thirty-five ranches in the community, whose livelihoods are sustainable with cattle, pasture and hay. Late comers, owning similar operations, include Sam Dinsdale, Lorraine Star and Furnette McDowell. Star and McDowell own the Brewer Ranch and the Wyman Ranch respectively. Names, faces, memories and places are not easily forgotten. One of the Kittredge clan moved away; but was not forgotten. His name is Bill, son of Oscar, grandson of the well respected cattle baron. The number two Bill, also left the ranching business, at an early age. He became a writer, author and college professor in Missoula, Montana.

60

Maurice and Mary Lou Emery have made their home in both Arizona and the Coast of Oregon for several years. The Metropolitan areas near Phoenix and Mesa have approximately the same problems as any large city. Waiting in line for gasoline, groceries and for seating in restaurants was tiring. The line at the post office to buy a postage stamp was really offensive. The air overhead was filled with a substance like smog. Relocating from Mesa, Arizona in 1995 to Wickenburg, Arizona, was their next move. In Wickenburg, they found that the air was free of smog, the traffic was tolerable and the lines at the post office and restaurants were practically non existent. They decided they would spend the winter months in Wickenburg and the summer months in the Northwest. They would, in this way, have the best of both the Northwest and Wickenburg.

Wickenburg, Arizona is approximately fifty miles from the Metropolitan Area in and around Phoenix, Arizona. Wickenburg was founded by a German Immigrant, Henry Wickenburg. Mr. Wickenburg was born in 1819. He came to the United States in 1847 and found his way to this area in 1863. His mining claim, near Vulture Peak, was developed and many millions of dollars of gold were mined prior to the closing of the mine in the early 1940's. The site is presently nothing more than an historic site; with falling down buildings. However, a visit and peek of yesteryear can be seen several days a week, just twelve miles from Wickenburg. Worldwide, geologists claim only a very small fraction of gold has ever been found. Those looking for gold in a desert, would be better advised to bring along a dry rocker rather than a wet sluice box. Gold bearing ores, heavy as they are, needed a rail road for moving ore. The "Peavine" railroad from Ashfork, Arizona to Phoenix passed through Wickenburg. This enabled the mine to ship its ore to various places for processing. A wooden structure was built for a train depot in the down town area in 1895. The former depot is and has been used by the Wickenburg Chamber of Commerce since 1987. For many years Wickenburg was known as "The Dude Ranch Capital of the World." Gold Rush Days in February, and resorts for winter visitors abound. A famous rodeo is held every year. Western attire can be found in several haberdasheries.

61

What is a senior citizen? Who is one? A senior citizen is one who was here prior to the population explosion. We were here before radios and television. We were here before U F O's and panty hose. Credit cards, radar, polio shots, dacron and florescent lights were unknown. Ball point pens, antibiotics, and drip dry clothing were non-existent. Many improvements, too numerous to mention, are graciously accepted. We were here before Bill and Hillary. We were here before George W. and Laura. Coeds never wore slacks; school girls wore black bloomers from their waist to their knees. Boys wore knee pants and button shoes. Bugs were small insects and were not Volkswagens, closets were for clothes, not for coming out of. Pot was for cooking; not something you smoked! ice makers, disposable diapers, vitamins and jeeps were in the foreseeable future for those looking ahead. Alaska and Hawaii had not yet become the forty-ninth and fiftieth states. Men never wore ear rings, grandmas never wore shorts, cowboys never wore baseball caps. We are today's senior citizens, a hardy group; when you think of how our world has changed. We are capable of making these adjustments and we will.

This "happy wanderer" on this 4th day of December, 2002, has minimal commitments. He must finalize this story encompassing a total of eighty-six-years. From the beginning of this story to the present time, he has found his life has been rewarding, sometimes complicated and obviously educational. He wants to return to "Lone Pine" and plant a pine tree to replace the one that served the ranch. Standing tall, it was a landmark for many, many years. A new tree would be most appropriate. It too, in time, would serve as a landmark and be greatly appreciated by the third and fourth generations As time passes, the fourth generation may, or may not, inhabit the ranch. Passersby would appreciate a tree standing in the forefront of this magnificent landscape. The sun and the moon glowing brilliantly as both descend behind the rim rocks, above the ranch home and out-buildings.

The End

0-595-28541-4

www.ingramcontent.com/pod-product-compliance
Lightning Source LLC
Chambersburg PA
CBHW020252290526
45784CB00003B/1223